"Growing Up" Teaching

"Growing Up" Teaching

FROM PERSONAL KNOWLEDGE TO PROFESSIONAL PRACTICE

Frances Schoonmaker

Teachers College, Columbia University
New York and London

Published by Teachers College Press, 1234 Amsterdam Avenue, New York, NY 10027

Portions of Chapters 1 and 4 are from "Promise and Possibility: Learning to Teach," by Frances Schoonmaker, 1998, *Teachers College Record, 99*(3), pp. 559–591. Reprinted with editorial modifications by permission.

Library of Congress Cataloging-in-Publication Data

Schoonmaker, Frances, 1941–
   "Growing up" teaching : From personal knowledge to professional practice / Frances Schoonmaker.
     p. cm.
   Includes bibliographical references and index.
   ISBN 0-8077-4271-6 (cloth : alk. paper) — ISBN 0-8077-4270-8 (pbk. : alk. paper)
    1. Teachers—Training of—United States—Case studies. I. Title.

  LB1715 .S33 2002
  370'.71'1—dc21   2002020296

ISBN 0-8077-4270-8 (paper)
ISBN 0-8077-4271-6 (cloth)

Printed on acid-free paper
Manufactured in the United States of America

09 08 07 06 05 04 03 02   8 7 6 5 4 3 2 1

To my first and best teachers:
Mom and Dad, Warren and Bruce
And my later, but no less important teacher:
Liesl

Contents

Preface

I dwell in Possibility
A fairer house than Prose,
More numerous of windows,
Superior of doors.
                    —Emily Dickinson

THIS STORY, a true one, is about possibilities. The story is about Kay and how she has learned to teach. It follows her career for nearly a decade, because she did not learn to teach all at once. We enter Kay's story when she begins a graduate-level teacher-preparation program. Her growing self-knowledge as a teacher, her beliefs about teaching and learning, and how these are reconstructed over time are all essential parts of the story.

Today, by all accounts, Kay is a teacher leader whose colleagues hold her in high regard. She had the benefit of a broadly conceived teacher-preparation program that emphasized deliberative, or thoughtful and reflective, teacher leadership. In addition to two semesters of student teaching, Kay spent a full year as an intern in a professional development school (PDS) during its pilot year and taught there for 9 years. As the book was beginning to take shape, Kay changed jobs, marking a new phase in her career. As Kay moves from the complex, urban environment of city schools to a school district in the metropolitan area near extended family, she reflects on her career from a new context and we reflect along with her.

Her possibilities are our possibilities as we think about some of the serious and perplexing questions that face schools. Among these are how to strengthen the link between knowledge of teaching and learning and classroom practice, how to get teacher education to "stick" once teachers are in the field, how to support teacher growth and development over time, and how to attract and retain academically able teachers. As we look at snapshots of Kay over the course of her career, it becomes more apparent how teachers construct personal theory out of a dialectic between personal knowledge, teacher education knowledge, and practical experience. This dialectic is so powerful that the university must pay particular attention to it if preservice preparation is to have a lasting effect.

In far too many cases, teacher preparation does not seem to have a lasting effect. Perhaps this is so because teacher education has not squared with what teacher education students already know. It is small wonder that university-based teacher education is being seriously questioned and challenged. If university-based teacher preparation is to have a role in the future, the university must come to terms with the key role that personal knowledge plays in learning and recognize that knowledge must be co-constructed if it is to have lasting meaning.

Furthermore, teacher education programs must take a long-term view of how teachers learn their craft and work with schools to provide a more holistic experience. There must be an organic connection between schools and universities in which the boundaries are permeable. Teachers, teacher educators, and neophyte teachers can then interact around issues of curriculum and teaching. The process of learning to teach should be recognized as a process of continuous reconstruction of experience that requires support over time. We see this in Kay's story. Her possibilities become our possibility for a deeper understanding of what it means to learn how to teach.

Kay's story is told through her own memories, papers she wrote while she was studying to become a teacher, her student teaching journal, observations of her in action with children and student teachers, and conversations. While it is her story, it is not her story alone. Other perspectives on Kay come from her student teachers—when they were in her classroom and years later from their vantage point as successful teachers—and by contrasting her with other teachers. But Kay remains at the center.

As the person putting together the story, I have tried to remain in the background. My reluctance to use the first person, except for occasional mentions, has to do with the fact that while I feel a part of the story—I have been Kay's teacher, supervised student teachers in her classroom, and been her colleague when she was clinical faculty—the story is not about me and my struggles as a teacher educator. It is about the possibilities inherent in how Kay is learning to teach.

I have had the good fortune to have the best of research assistants helping me with various stages of this 10-year-long project: Stacey Girodano, Jennifer Goodwin, Christine Clayton, Penny Howell, and Victoria Frelow. Thanks to Shabiya Wahabodeen and Jo Ellen Thomas of the Department of Curriculum and Teaching for their help. I am also grateful to Teachers College (TC) for a Research Fellowship to work on the manuscript in 2000–2001. And many thanks to colleagues in the preservice program at

TC—A. Lin Goodwin, Celia Oyler, and Anne Sabatini—and to the many TC preservice students, cooperating teachers, and PDS faculty who, over the years, have taught me so much about teacher preparation. Finally, and most significantly, I am grateful to Karen Siegl-Smith, "Kay," whose unflagging goodwill and professional curiosity made the book possible.

Pseudonyms are used for all teachers throughout the book. It was Kay's preference to use a pseudonym to allow herself some distance for reflection.

ဆ 1 ര

Promise and Possibility

> If I have all the intelligence [people] say I do, then the children who will make the future deserve to get the benefit of this.
>
> —Kay, August 1989

WHEN WE first meet Kay, she is one of about 80 students in the preservice program in early childhood and elementary education at Teachers College (TC). She is smart, but so is everybody else in the program. She is quiet—she seems to listen to other people. There is a sparkle in her brown eyes, and she has a hearty laugh that carries across the room. She has expressed an interest in being placed in the college's new professional development school (PDS) for student teaching.

THE PROMISE

Like almost everyone else in the program, Kay is a liberal arts graduate. She decided to become a teacher sometime during her sophomore year at Cornell University. Kay had always loved school. It was a place she liked to be and where she felt successful, and "it occurred to me that the jobs I had held as a summer camp counselor were the ones I enjoyed most and were the ones that never seemed like work; they were fun."

Deciding to teach was one of many barriers standing between Kay and a promising career. The first was facing the attitudes of family, friends, and college professors who advised her to look for a profession that would be more economically rewarding and more "intellectually" challenging. But Kay was determined.

Although there are attractive alternative routes into teaching for college graduates, which would have placed her directly in the classroom, she sets her sites on a graduate-level teacher education program. After her experience as a camp counselor for 6-year-old boys, Kay was convinced

1

that she wanted to go into the classroom prepared. It took "all the patience and creativity I could muster" to stay on top of things at camp.

Confirming the Decision to Teach

Once Kay had made up her mind to teach, she looked for hands-on experience to confirm her decision. During her last 2 years as an undergraduate at Cornell, she took a position as group leader for 23 7-year-olds in a community center in downtown Ithaca, New York. The decision had a strong impact on future choices. It was her first experience in an inner-city setting, working with minority students and staff. She came face to face with the social and economic discrepancies between the lives of children at the center and her own privileged upbringing in a suburban, upper-middle-class, largely Jewish community.

> The children provided me a chance to see how different back-grounds can cause different reactions to experiences while at the same time turn out children with amazingly similar concerns and actions. By meeting the parents and inquiring about the children's home lives, I really saw how different the childhood experience can be.

Kay took advantage of the opportunity to visit a school in the neighborhood and talk with teachers. She remembers that they were welcoming and used a lot of new methods that appealed to her, such has whole language for reading instruction.

Later, Kay became a tutorial supervisor in the after-school program. She had to develop the program "from scratch without anyone around with previous experience." Just getting the children to attend was an enormous challenge. Finding resources, given the low budget of the community program, presented another. But getting children to do their homework was "the challenge that I found most discouraging." Like the teachers described by Michael Knapp and colleagues (1995) in "high-poverty classrooms," she, too, wondered why it was so hard.

Emerging Inclinations

Already, both preexistent and emergent theory about teaching and learning are evident in her thinking. Kay discovers that "most children would rather play sports or do arts and crafts than something academic." Just as she wants work for herself that does not "seem like work," she wants children to enjoy themselves. She begins to create games and contests to get the children to come for tutoring and to keep them interested. She also forms a close relationship with three children from a family in the area, stopping by their home on her way to or from work when she can. In doing so, she learns about the need for teachers to understand and respect children's lives outside school.

Kay has discovered the importance of creating an environment that nurtures active learning. She believes learning should be fun. She shows an inclination to experiment. And she has a growing appreciation of the social context of schooling as she learns that children's families and school communities have an impact on school experiences. As we will see in following Kay's career, these ideals are enduring ingredients in her construction of self as a teacher. Kay is highly motivated. She wants to work in an urban school and shows promise of becoming the kind of professional who will work to overcome the "pedagogy of poverty," a pedagogy that focuses on authoritarian control, described as characteristic of urban schools (Haberman, 1991).

TEACHER DEVELOPMENT AS SOCIALIZATION

Given this hopeful beginning, what can we anticipate for Kay's future career in education? The literature on the effectiveness of teacher preparation has become robust in the past decade, and while conclusions are not uniform, research informs us about the career trajectories of prospective teachers in a number of important ways.

Characterizing Typical Development

Teacher development may be seen as socially constructed. Teachers tend to grow along similar lines, as developmental stage theory suggests, but this growth and development reflect the powerful force of schools as agencies of socialization. So potent is the process of socialization that the effects of teacher preparation tend to be washed out when neophyte teachers enter the school. Kay is likely to develop as a teacher along particular lines that suggest four significant trends and result in a high rate of teacher dropout among the academically able.

First, we know that Kay's own preconceptions and implicit theories about teaching and learning will play a major part in her development as a teacher (Clark, 1988; Hollingsworth, 1989; Lortie, 1975; Zeichner & Liston, 1987). Kay's implicit theoretical perspective must be teased out of the statements that she makes about herself as teacher and about children and schools. These might be described as *theoretical inclinations,* and they are precursors to theory. Theoretical inclinations are comprised of an assortment of beliefs. As Christopher Clark (1988) points out, "teachers' implicit theories tend to be eclectic aggregations of cause–effect propositions from many sources, rules of thumb, generalizations drawn from personal experience, beliefs, values, biases, and prejudices" (p. 6).

We can postulate that as Kay's beliefs become more known to us, contradictions within her own "eclectic aggregation" will emerge. Furthermore, while the views she articulates seem compatible with constructivist theory, it is likely that her understanding is restricted and focused on a few specific kinds of activity, such as the experiences she describes in her tutoring program (see Calderhead & Robson, 1991; Kagan, 1992). While she may be predisposed to act in particular ways, as Alberto J. Rodriguez (1993) observed, "a disposition to act is not the same thing as acting on a disposition" (p. 214). Like most teachers, Kay is likely to become so involved in the rapidly paced life of the classroom that she will give little time to the kind of deliberation envisioned by reformers of teacher education and schools and that her actions will often be inconsistent with her professed beliefs.

Most of Kay's elementary and secondary education was in traditional classrooms—and she loved school. Contradictory images of teaching and learning drawn from this experience will reside along with Kay's nascent constructivist theory. In fact, judging from the literature, we can expect that Kay's prior experiences in school, or what Daniel Lortie called the "apprenticeship of observation," will be more powerful than her teacher-preparation program. If Kay's teacher education program is typical, the influence of this prior "apprenticeship" will persist, contributing to her development of the very authoritarian teaching practices she deplores (Britzman, 1986; Goodman, 1988; McNeil, 1986; Tabachnick & Zeichner, 1984; Zeichner & Tabachnick, 1981).

Second, if Kay's development as a teacher is typical, she will leave her teacher-preparation program with the conviction that theory is abstract and unrelated to the realities of teaching. Kay will perpetuate the common notion that theory and practice are largely unrelated. She will be convinced that it is in the classroom where one "really learns" to teach, and her student-teaching experience will be seen as the most powerful part of her preparation (Britzman, 1986; Lortie, 1975). Kay will probably "internalize the pervasive cultural belief that experience makes the teacher" (Britzman, 1986, p. 447). More than likely, her student-teaching experience will negate coursework at the university, leading her to set it aside for practical activities, reinforcing her prior experience and a utilitarian perspective, even if the preparation program promotes reflective practice (Zeichner, 1980; Zeichner, 1984). Despite her keen intelligence, motivation, and what she will learn at the university, Kay is unlikely to contribute in any significant way to school reform because she will find student teaching more compelling than her coursework and student teaching will serve to further entrench present practices. Kay will learn to do what her cooperating teacher does (Goodlad, 1997), and this will, more likely than not, be conservative.

Third, despite Kay's motivation to be a caring teacher in the nation's most challenging schools, she will become more concerned about control than about issues of teaching and learning. Her "natural inclinations to be rational and caring" will "give way to teaching methods that are authoritative and promote competition" (Arnstine, 1990, p. 24), in effect maintaining and reproducing cultural myths related to domination and social control in schooling (Britzman, 1986). Most schools are organized along hierarchical lines, with social control as an important classroom dynamic (see Apple, 1982). If children are not socialized into forms of education that emphasize collaboration, respect for each other, responsibility for materials, and interactive processes, they resist when nonauthoritarian practices are introduced. Resistance becomes a classroom-management problem, which disturbs the school ethos. Under such conditions, Kay's initial readiness to become a teacher who continues to be a student of teaching will give way to an unreflective emphasis on doing what works—usually understood to be authoritarian discipline and curriculum practices.

Fourth, even if her teacher-preparation program succeeds in helping her to develop reflective practices, Kay would find them incompatible with the demands of most schools. What if Kay's program were able to help her penetrate and reconstruct prior images; be a critical, reflective participant in her student-teaching experience; and develop an understanding of the social and political realities of schools? She would still be unprepared to deal with the realities of schooling because in most schools where she is likely to begin her career, the goals of education and schooling would be incompatible with her preparation. As Haberman (1991) argues, "there is a pervasive, fundamental, irreconcilable difference between the motivation of those who select themselves to become teachers and the demands of urban teaching" (p. 291).

Wildman and Niles (1987) point out:

> Expectations inherent in teacher reflection are difficult to justify, given the demands of schools, because they are counter to a world in which (a) the goals of schooling can be narrowly defined in terms of basic academic skills and achievement scores, (b) the means to obtain those goals can be clearly specified from research, and (c) the teachers can be collected in large groups to hear about the procedures they will be expected to follow. (p. 30)

Finally, Kay, as an academically able student, is likely to leave teaching within the first 5 years. Suppose Kay does survive all the hurdles of teacher preparation, enters teaching in the urban school setting where she desires to teach, and manages to counteract the "pedagogy of poverty" and the vagaries and vicissitudes of school reform. Will she survive as a career teacher? While we know that Kay not only survives, but also has a successful career, at entry the odds are against her staying with teaching. Academically able students are less likely to choose teaching as a career, take teaching jobs if they do complete a preparation program, and stay with teaching as a career for more than 5 years if they actually enter the profession (Murnane, 1991).

The prospects for Kay are not welcoming. Instead of offering her a bright future, the realities of teacher preparation and life in schools are such that she seems to be at risk of dropping out of the profession at almost every point along the way.

Being at Risk

Kay's "survival" in teacher preparation and as a new teacher is important for its own sake, as she strives to achieve a personal goal. But the fact that she is at risk of dropping out or failing to become the teacher she hopes to be has a broader meaning because, as an academically able and liberally educated college graduate, Kay is representative of those we most want and seem to be least able to recruit and retain in the profession. Today, she is a veteran teacher, into her 10th year in the classroom. Her practice is characterized by deliberative leadership (Zumwalt, 1982). Colleagues describe her as "solid." And she has already mentored new student teachers and beginning teachers in her school, has been deeply involved in PDS action research on the role of the cooperating teacher, and has served as a member of the PDS clinical faculty. What are we to make of Kay's survival and success in the profession given the backdrop of discouraging expectations for candidates who match her profile?

For teacher educators, the most confounding barrier to promising teachers is likely to be prior experiences and beliefs or personal knowledge. The fact that personal knowledge seems to trump preparation knowledge suggests that teacher preparation is ineffectual. And it feeds into the public notion that anybody can teach. However, Gary Griffin (1986) argues that while many studies claim that formal teacher preparation has little impact on the powerful influence of prior experience, this conclusion "probably rests upon the inadequacy of particular teacher education programs of study" (p. 2). By looking closely at Kay's experience as a student in a "broadly conceived" program and following her career development, we can learn more about how to overcome the impact of prior images and other significant barriers that place bright young people who choose to teach at risk of leaving the profession or being negatively shaped by it.

Challenging the Expected

Over the years since her graduation, I have spent many hours in Kay's classroom, primarily working with student teachers. We have served on countless PDS committees and attended preservice program planning meetings together. It was 6 years after her graduation from the program that we began to explore her own sense of how she has developed as a teacher. By this time, she had made it past the first 5 years, during which the odds had it that she would drop out of the profession.

Kay recalls her first weeks of being responsible for her own classroom, contrasting her experience to that of colleagues who were graduates of another teacher-preparation program, one with a strong, progressive–practical orientation. These colleagues were representative of their school's sentiment regarding how teachers ought to be prepared. While Kay felt uncertainty and confusion, they seemed to know exactly what to do. "I'd look at them and I'd think, 'Well, that'd be nice, if I knew exactly what to do!'" It took her several years to appreciate what she had learned. "I've figured it out, you know! That's the difference." Figuring out is a key ingredient in her experimental mindset about teaching. She tells a friend who had just been admitted to the TC program, "When you first come out of TC, you're going to think, 'What'd they do for me? Nothing!' ... Then later on, 5 years down the road, you're gonna say, 'No, I really did get a lot out of it.'"

When asked what she thought we most wanted from her while she was a preservice student, Kay replied, "Definitely to reflect. Definitely to reflect. I think it was to reflect on your teaching and constantly grow." But, she says, "I don't know how you can say whether—if I would be able to label my teaching as theoretical *or* practical."

Kay's student-teaching journal shows that from the very beginning of her program, she made connections between what the school referred to as the "theoretical stuff at TC" and her more "practical and real" student-teaching experiences. These connections did not occur by chance, however, nor did becoming a deliberative teacher leader just happen. Reflective teacher preparation requires attention to what the research literature refers to as *elements* such as thinking processes and *strategies* for developing teacher reflection.

REFLECTIVE TEACHER PREPARATION

The way the preservice program at TC attempted to shape Kay's development as a deliberative (thoughtful, reflective) teacher leader is grounded in the broader research literature on teacher reflection. Even the most cursory review of this literature leads to the realization that reflection, like beauty, may be in the eye of the beholder. While teacher educators seem to agree that getting fledgling teachers to reflect is a good thing, the way reflection is described and studied as well as the ends toward which teacher reflection is aimed seem much less clear (Bolin, 1988; Smyth, 1989; Sparks-Langer & Colton, 1991; Tom, 1985; Zeichner, 1987).

The Research Base for Teacher Reflection

Some teacher educators seek to bring about cognitive change in preservice students to enable them to be more specific in their knowledge of pupil learning and context variables (Hollingsworth, 1989). There are a variety of ways in which teacher educators who see reflection as a cognitive process attempt to bring about these changes. Practices range from implementation of specific techniques that promote reflective thought (e.g., Pultorak, 1993; Sparks-Langer & Simmons, 1990) to emphasis on decision making about practice (Yinger & Clark, 1981). Other teacher educators and researchers focus on the knowledge base for teaching (Shulman, 1987).

Ends and means differ within clusters of research on teacher reflection. For example, researchers interested in strategies that delineate steps toward reflection have applied Van Manen's (1977) levels of reflectivity, following the recommendations of Zeichner and Liston (1987) in strikingly different ways. Van Manen's levels of reflectivity have been utilized to analyze reflection in highly formulaic programs; for example, Pultorak (1993) describes a program that taught both assertive discipline and the UCLA model of lesson planning and supervision. Van Manen's work has also been applied to study programs more emancipatory in structure and goals, as in the case of the Wisconsin model (Zeichner & Liston, 1987).

For other researchers, reflection is a process by which teachers make more intelligent decisions about teaching strategies (e.g., Cruickshank & Applegate, 1981; Hollingsworth, 1989). This process may or may not include a consideration of how particular strategies may be context-specific, making it difficult for new teachers to apply strategies in a context different from the one in which they were learned (Hollingsworth, 1989; Lampert & Clark, 1990). Still other teacher educators see reflection as a process for emancipation of the student teacher from oppressive structures within society. These are programs focused on reflection—often on the preparation program itself and the student teacher's own autobiography—as a means to social ends (e.g., Beyer, 1984; Smyth, 1989). John Smyth (1989) suggests:

> Reflection can, therefore, vary from a concern with the micro aspects of the teaching learning process and subject matter knowledge, to macro concerns

about political/ethical principles underlying teaching and the relationship of schooling to the wider institutions and hierarchies of society. (p. 4)

Regardless of emphasis and interest, however, most researchers recognize that teacher reflection is a complex area of study.

To summarize, three elements of teacher reflection have been the subject of study:

1. The cognitive, relating to information processing and decision making by teachers
2. The substantive, or what drives thinking, including experiences, goals, values, and social implications
3. Teachers' narratives, or their interpretations of events occurring within their particular contexts (Sparks-Langer & Colton, 1991)

Sparks-Langer and Colton see the second as critical if we are to understand what actually happens when teachers engage in reflective practice.

Turning to *strategies*, Zeichner (1987) identifies three ways in which one might differentiate among strategies for preparation of reflective teachers:

1. The level at which intervention is directed
2. The degree to which steps are delineated toward reflection
3. The extent to which a theoretical perspective is identified

It is a common assumption in both pre- and inservice teacher education that teachers should be more reflective about their professional practice. But the research literature on teacher preparation suggests that there is little agreement among teacher educators about the nature of reflection and how it ought to be developed. Therefore, goals and approaches of teacher education programs vary widely.

A Social-Cultural Orientation to Teacher Preparation

The TC preservice program in which Kay enrolled describes its mission as preparing academically able, liberal arts graduates for deliberative practice as leaders in the profession of teaching. Expanding on Zeichner's (1987) list of strategies may illuminate the way this mission is enacted in relation to teacher reflection:

1. *The level at which intervention is directed, which may range from program revision to attempts to influence structure of schools and teaching.* In the preservice program intervention is directed at multiple levels. Specific

assignments are given to students to promote reflection; for example, they are required to keep student-teaching journals (see Bolin, 1988, 1990, for discussion of the dialogue journal as a tool for student reflection).

Continuous revision of the program occurs, following a collaborative planning model. Promoting teacher educator reflection is as important to us as promoting student teacher reflection. That is, we believe that it would not be possible for teacher educators who are not self-critical and thoughtful about their work to promote these qualities in student teachers. Preparation and ongoing meetings with student-teaching supervisors also occur during both semesters in which students are in field placements. The TC program attempts to influence the broader context of schools and teaching through the PDS and a cooperating schools network with teachers and administrators of the several schools where we place student teachers. Network meetings have examined issues as wide-ranging as how to welcome new student teachers and goals of particular methods courses they take to complete their program. Occasionally participants have organized to do action research on topics of interest, such as how to support student teacher development.

2. *The degree to which steps are delineated toward reflection.* In the preservice program, steps are seen as less important than developing a context and climate for reflection through activities and experiences based on the dispositions we foster through program themes. Our intent is to help students move toward serious and thoughtful questioning and understanding of their own perceptions, actions, feelings, values, and cultural biases as these relate to the practical work that is most compelling to them. "How tos," to borrow Dewey's term, are less important than developing ways of observing, questioning, and inventing.

3. *The extent to which a theoretical perspective is identified.* The preservice program respects a variety of theoretical perspectives on teaching and learning, while building on a progressive tradition that is social constructivist in philosophy. This is described in program literature as follows:

> The Preservice Program also reflects the pluralism of Teachers College; students in the program study a wide variety of approaches to education rather than a single approach.
>
> Our stance is that there is no single truth in education but there are many realities. Each of us has the right to choose our own (educated) platform, but we who are teacher educators have the obligation to introduce our students to the spectrum

of alternatives and help them to look at the important differences among approaches. Because there is no one clearly superior way to engage in educating children, teachers must constantly set hypotheses and test them, searching for the best way to teach each individual child and group of children. Such teaching lacks the safety and predictability of the "tried and true" approach, and requires individuals who understand the limitations of fixed formulas and who enjoy reaching out into the unpredictable world created by the diversity and the uniqueness of each child and each group of children.

We want our students to understand that forms of knowledge, including self-reflection and questioning, are socially and culturally constructed. When any approach to curriculum and teaching becomes a formula to be applied in every school, it becomes a form of social domination.

THE POSSIBILITY

The way reflection is viewed in the preservice program at TC is compatible with those approaches that focus on meaning-making through reflection on self in relation to others, social and cultural context, and consequences. This is not unlike views described by Elliott (1976–77) and by Zeichner and Liston (1987). Elliott talks about reflection as a process of "self-monitoring" in which "one becomes aware of one's situation and one's own role as an agent in it" (p. 5). Zeichner and Liston describe goals for preparation of teachers "who are both willing and able to reflect on the origins, purposes, and consequences of their actions, as well as on the material and ideological constraints and encouragements embedded in the classroom, school, and societal contexts in which they work" (1987, p. 23).

In a paper written at the conclusion of a course on the role of the cooperating teacher in teacher education, 4 years after graduating from the program, Kay wrote, "There seems to be an enormous amount to think about and explore. This thinking seems to be leading up to an enormous need for reform, both in my personal theories and in the society values and structures all aspects of education rely on." This inclination and ability to question personal as well as school and societal structures is what we hope will increasingly characterize all students who graduate from the preservice program as they continue to develop themselves as teachers.

Three of the barriers to development of reflective teachers that are identified in the research literature were evident in Kay's crucial first semester of student teaching and serve as organizing categories in reviewing her experience:

1. The powerful role of *preconceptions and implicit theories*
2. The focus on practical experience while deemphasizing *integration of theory and practice*
3. The tendency for concern about *exerting control in the classroom* to supersede motivation to be caring

While Kay may have been predisposed to being shaped as a deliberative teacher leader, there were significant aspects of the preservice program that addressed each of these "negatives" and moved Kay along. This is not to suggest any lack of agency on Kay's part; ultimately her development is as an individual within a complex social and cultural nexus.

The role of preconceptions and implicit theories is explored in this and the following two chapters. Chapter 4 turns to integration of theory and practice and the concern for classroom control. And, in chapters to follow, we will see how each of the barriers to development of reflective practice is surmounted in Kay's career development.

Surfacing Preconceptions and Implicit Theories

Prior to her first week of student teaching, Kay began the preservice core, a group of courses clustered into one time block that is planned, co-taught, and assessed by preservice faculty. Students take the two-semester core concurrent with student teaching. When Kay was in the program, students spent three mornings and one full day in their student-teaching placement. The core is designed to be the integrating center of the program, though most students experience student teaching as much more powerful than either coursework (e.g., foundations, electives) or the core. During the first session, Kay was challenged to look inward at her own elementary school experiences and outward to the broader social context in which teaching takes place. The intent is to initiate a dialectical relationship between autobiography and curriculum context and practice.

The "inward look" draws on students' *personal knowledge*, a theme that runs through two semesters of the core. Learning activities and experiences that draw on personal knowledge are intended to help students bring prior experience to a conscious level and examine it so that they may intentionally critique and reconstruct it. Kay becomes deeply engaged in the first core session as students are asked to construct a symbol that represents one of their most positive memories from elementary school. Symbols are shared with a small group of peers. The room, which had become quiet as students focused on their own recollections, becomes animated. Peer groups are asked to think about what their experiences have in common and what this might tell them about teaching. From these discussions, a list is generated. They notice that "the activities were hands-on," "they brought positive recognition," "they were extracurricular experiences," and the like. In guiding the discussions, faculty tie these reports of experience to knowledge about teaching and learning, pointing out that our own experiences can teach us a great deal about what children need and want. Negative experiences are examined in a similar way. (In Chapters 2 and 3, I explore the significance of early recollections.)

During the first core session, the outward look is presented as a mini-lecture in which students are introduced to the idea of studying classrooms, children, and schools. *Social, political, and contextual knowledge* are introduced and become recurrent themes. Again, students are invited to think about how their own prior experience as elementary school students and their own experiences with racial, ethnic, social, and gender diversity can be instructive. Given the diverse population of students they will meet in the urban schools where they student-teach and our program's commitment to social justice and equity, *cultural diversity* becomes an important and prominent theme.

Throughout the session Kay and other student teachers spend part of the time working in groups. As part of the core, they take a course on models of teaching that emphasizes group discussion and cooperative learning, equipping them with *organizational knowledge* that will assist them in working with children and adults.

By the end of the first core session, the four broad program themes of *personal knowledge, organizational knowledge, social, political, and contextual knowledge,* and *pedagogical knowledge* have been introduced through specific activities, the physical arrangement of the core instructional space, working in small groups, the faculty's team approach to their instruction, and "mini-lecture" content related to classrooms and models of teaching. Each of these themes is developed through a variety of activities and experiences throughout the two-semester block.

Kay's reaction to the first core session is strong and positive. She writes:

I loved talking about our personal experiences in elementary school. My early schooling was a very positive time for me, but even so I can think of things I would like not to happen to other children. The others' experiences added more to my list, and they reminded me that teaching is a great deal more than just academics.

Deconstructing Personal Knowledge

Kay's personal knowledge comes into play from the first, revealing contradictory images and beliefs. While the contradictions are more apparent to an outsider reading her work than they are to Kay, they become more conscious to her as she is required to examine them in her student-teaching journal (read by her college supervisor) and in periodic reflection papers written for the core. Without such deliberate intervention, it is unlikely that her personal knowledge will be conscious or that it will do more than subvert her preparation program, given the fast-paced work of student teaching. Without intervention, prior images are likely to lie dormant until she begins teaching and finds herself setting aside "academic" preparation for ways that seem more realistic or "right," not because they have proven to be effective, but because they are drawn from older patterns of response and feeling.

Ideas and inclinations to respond are drawn from personal knowledge and often present themselves as "shoulds." One *should* know how to teach; one *should* have a reservoir of knowledge and expertise sufficient to meet any and all demands, even as a beginner; and one *should* learn more from being in the classroom than from studying about the classroom—to name some powerful "shoulds." Britzman (1986) speaks of these as cultural myths to which student teachers unconsciously subscribe: "(1) Everything depends on the teacher; (2) the teacher is the expert; (3) teachers are 'self-made' " (p. 448).

Kay's belief that the teacher should be an expert surfaces during her first week of student teaching in a first-grade classroom. After her first day in the student-teaching classroom, Kay writes in her journal that "the task of getting them all reading and writing and spelling, while not letting the ones who already know how to get bored" is enormous. "Everything is overwhelming," she writes on day 2, "I feel like I have so much to learn and that I'll never know enough to take on a class myself." This notion, according to Britzman (1986), breeds fear that one will never know enough to teach and reinforces the view of the teacher as an autonomous individual and knowledge as something to be delivered.

Janet, her cooperating teacher, does more than reassure her. "Janet's wonderful about explaining anything to me and she listens to my ideas as well. She's really letting me take a part in the planning of the daily program as well as participating throughout the day." By the second day,

Kay is using the term *we* in talking about the classroom: "Janet feels that we can slow down. We'll work longer on one lesson and do more with it." She is part of a team. Janet has challenged not only the notion that teachers are expert but also the idea that teaching is something that occurs in isolation from other adults (Britzman, 1986; Lortie, 1975). Janet lets Kay in on her thinking about planning and asks for ideas. Kay is not waiting to take over the classroom as a solo performance; she is experiencing teaching as a collaborative process.

This initial collaborative experience holds throughout the semester. In her mid-semester evaluation of Kay's student teaching, Janet writes, "I am reminded of the co-teacher position Kay has in our classroom. She is a remarkable student teacher—confident, relaxed, intelligent, creative, organized, and kind." Kay's supervisor notes on the final evaluation, "Watching Kay work with Janet was perhaps the most exciting part of being Kay's supervisor. They were clearly a team, two professionals that respected each other's strengths and weaknesses."

Teaching as a collaborative endeavor is strengthened by the PDS effort. Teachers at the elementary school site have agreed that those involved in PDS work will form grade-level pairs to jointly plan a curriculum. Kay is also witnessing schoolwide collaboration as the faculty struggle to establish their identity as a PDS and determine goals and policies. She writes on her final evaluation of student teaching, "I have interacted with many of the other first-grade teachers. I feel we have discussed many things, which helped me a lot. I hope these relationships will continue."

As she enters the final weeks of first-semester student teaching, Kay is still describing collaborative planning. We recall, however, that Kay *loved* school. Her schooling was in traditional classrooms, reminding us that impressions from the two contexts (student teaching and past experience) do not match. While she is becoming aware of the contradiction between past experience and the orientation she is acquiring, as yet it is unlikely that Kay has begun to significantly reconstruct her own theories about teaching and learning.

CONCLUSION

As we have looked at Kay on the cusp of a promising career, we are in a position somewhat analogous to someone reading a mystery novel after having looked at the last chapter. We, like the reader, know that everything turns out splendidly, with the main character having circumvented the many obstacles between Chapter 1 and the end. We know that Kay survives entry into the profession and constructs a career that is personally meaningful and professionally successful. But, like the mystery novel reader, we do not know *how she did it*. At this point, what we *do* know is that Kay does not begin as a blank slate on which the teacher-preparation program inscribes its goals. She begins with a nascent theory informed by personal knowledge. Her ideals stand in marked contrast to the bleak research-based expectations for student teachers who match her profile as an academically able student. Helping Kay to become the deliberative teacher she is today was not a chance activity; rather, it involved intentional strategies to help her penetrate preconceptions and implicit theories, making connections between this personal knowledge and the university program. All of this was done in a context of meaning-making, framed by the social and cultural realities of teaching.

But how does Kay reconstruct personal knowledge? To understand how Kay begins to reconstruct personal knowledge, we look at the nature of prior images of teaching. We do this in the following chapters by examining Kay's early recollections of being a student along with those of teachers from other cultural contexts.

ഇ 2 ൠ

The Social Construction
of Personal Knowledge

I have a sister a year older, who obviously went to school a
year ahead of me. I was dying to go! I mean, when she left
in the morning, I would have a fit because I wasn't going!
That is my earliest memory: wanting to go to school.
                                              —Kay, May 2000

HOW TEACHERS deal with personal knowledge may determine the extent
to which they benefit from preservice preparation and, very likely, from
staff development. In the next two chapters, we begin to "unpack" some
of Kay's personal knowledge by examining her earliest recollections of
school. These recollections tell us what is most important to her and give
us clues about the construction of teacher knowledge as we compare them
to recollections of other teachers across cultural contexts.

KAY'S PERSONAL KNOWLEDGE

Kay remembers how much she wanted to go to school once her sister
got to go. She pauses, brow furrowed, quiet for a moment: "I'm trying
to think of the first positive memory—probably learning to read in kindergarten." She laughs. The memory seems to be coming alive for her.

Kay's face lights up as speaks. "I can remember sitting in a reading
group, reading 'Dick and Jane.' I can picture myself sitting at the round
table learning, learning to read, and being excited about that." She elabo-
rates, "It was tables. It was a half-day kindergarten. I don't remember
much other than the reading group and the fact there was stuff going on
at the table . . . I can't remember much else that was going on." Kay's
recollection is brief. But it is not random. There are no "chance memories"
(Adler, 1931/1964, p. 351).

In the compression and simplicity of this first memory, we gain a valuable picture of Kay's view of teaching and learning. This memory shows her first satisfactory integration of what happened at school and her attitude toward it.

Early recollections have long been seen as an important part of psychotherapy. Alfred Adler (1914/1964) is particularly associated with looking at early recollections, considering them one of "the most trustworthy approaches to the exploration of the personality" (pp. 327–328). Adler's psychology focuses on social interest and the life goals that individuals have in its pursuit.

In contrast to Freud's objective stance, Adler is subjective in orientation. He recognizes the influence of biological and environmental factors in development but sees the individual as goal oriented and choosing. And Adler's theory assumes that the individual cannot be understood apart from a social situation—the individual is *socially embedded.* "We refuse to recognize and examine an isolated human being" (Adler, 1926/1964, p. 2). For Adler, all significant problems in life are social problems and values are social values.

Exploring School Memories

For Kay, the starting point and immediate social context is sitting at a table, with a group, and learning to read.

> The only thing I know is that not everybody was in a reading group. It was kids they *deemed* as ready to learn to read. I don't think I realized that at the time, but I realize that in retrospect. That may have something to do with it, too, that not everybody got to be in a reading group. I know we sat in a small group around the table. I remember my teacher, Mrs. York. I can picture us with the books open, then when we were done, bringing them home to read to my parents. That would be my first positive memory about school.

We know from Kay's earlier comments that she was reared in a largely upper-middle-class, Jewish community on Long Island in New York. This, too, is part of her social construction.

It is of little consequence whether her early recollection is the very first event that can be remembered, rather than the one that spontaneously came to mind, or whether it is accurate or fictional. What is recalled suggests what is valued. How Kay interprets this first memory is more significant than the memory itself. In Adler's (1931/1964) words, "Memories are important only for what they are 'taken as'; for their interpretation and for their bearing on present and future life" (p. 352). Kay, thinking about her experience, comments.

> Of course I was really excited. It was fabulous that I was in the reading group. But the fact that two-thirds of the class didn't learn to read—not that they didn't learn to read, but weren't in a formal reading group—and only a third of the kids got to be? That is bizaar in retrospect! I was really happy to be the one who was singled out, not singled out, but with the group that was singled out.
>
> I can think about it in a positive way. It's about encouraging each kid and motivating them and making them feel special. Looking back, you should certainly try to do it without putting down the rest of the class. As a kid that is really what it was, being made to feel special, being made to . . . the expectations were high, it was like, "You can do this, you are ready for it."

Noticing the Patterns

Within this early memory and its present meaning for Kay, we can see the emergent pattern that was evident in her nascent theory upon entering the preservice program. It contains several key elements: The underlying theme is about getting to do something—learn something—which was special and fun in itself. Repeated throughout her first-semester journal is the idea that learning should be fun and rewarding—having books, learning to read them, and being singled out encapsulate this belief. The memory involves being acted upon by the teacher, or chosen to be at the reading table, and her own sense of satisfaction, but it is primarily a social activity, involving a community—sitting at tables and taking books home to read to parents are key elements. Her language moves from self to the group.

Based on this early memory, Kay's recommendation to herself as a teacher and to other teachers is to believe in children. She was made to believe in herself and wants all children to enjoy learning, have fun, and be challenged to believe in their own capabilities. We will see each of these as recurrent themes as we track Kay's development in the following chapters. They are the building blocks out of which her career has been shaped.

Helping Kay to recognize and deconstruct personal knowledge will help her in the process of reconstructing experience as she learns to teach. It will enable her to notice her own reactions to particular children, to curricula, and to inservice and staff development activities as she continues to learn on the job. But it will not necessarily equip her to understand the socially embedded nature of what her students know and what other teachers know.

The social "embeddedness" of our own personal knowledge makes it hard for us to recognize its powerful influence at any point in our lives. We take it for granted that the way we see things is the way they are, contributing to the hegemony, or domination, of those in power in a society. Identifying personal knowledge does not necessarily enable us to see how it is situated within social, cultural, and racial structures that define particular communities. For this reason, I believe it is instructive to juxtapose Kay's personal knowledge, as evidenced in her early recollections, with recollections of beginning and experienced teachers in three different national contexts where I have taught—the United States, China, and Japan. Comparing these cross-cultural recollections offers us a broader picture of the actual material out of which teacher beliefs and theories are constructed and how culture and context shape teacher beliefs.

OBSTRUCTIONS OR OPPORTUNITIES?

The significance of prior experiences in shaping teacher beliefs and practices has been well established in the literature on teacher education (Calderhead, 1996; Clark, 1988; Hollingsworth, 1989; Joram & Gabriele, 1998; Lortie, 1975; Maxson & Sindelar, 1998; Zeichner & Liston, 1987). *How* significant prior experiences are is difficult to determine and undoubtedly will vary with individual teachers. However, what Lortie (1975) pointed out years ago is apparently still true: The learning from many teacher education programs is simply set aside when neophyte teachers begin to teach. In fact, as we noted in Chapter 1, one of the barriers to becoming a successful teacher is that most teachers believe their university training is theoretical, abstract, and unrelated to the realities of teaching (Britzman, 1986; Zeichner, 1980, 1984). When university preparation is seen as unrelated to the realities of teaching, then alternative routes to teaching and apprenticeship models make sense. Preparation programs are seen as neither necessary nor desirable for teachers except as they furnish broad, liberal, and content preparation for teachers to take with them to the classroom.

Accessing Prior Experience

It is not surprising, then, that university-based teacher educators are troubled by the influence of prior beliefs and see them as obstructions to effective teacher preparation. Joram and Gabriele (1998), for example, argue that "these beliefs act as a gatekeeper to belief change throughout the teacher education program" (p. 177). Maxson and Sindelar (1998) suggest that the implication of this research adds "another dimension to the call for more attention to teacher beliefs' research" (p. 7).

Teacher educators have experimented with a variety of strategies to deal with prior images with "mixed results" (Joram & Gabriele, 1998, p. 175). The challenge appears to be how to access prior beliefs in order to make teachers, particularly student teachers, aware of them so that "the teacher educator may simultaneously attempt to mold the students' images into the theoretical shape desired by a specific teacher education program" (Maxson & Sindelar, 1998, p. 6).

It seems that the field of teacher education is moving toward greater understanding and ordering of the cognitive development of teachers. A taxonomy of the cognitive processes or mechanisms of teacher development promises to show how individuals move through natural stages toward maturity. Such an ordering would permit teacher educators to explore and manipulate these mechanisms of development, including the teacher's own belief systems, through (1) creating disequilibrium as the teacher sees the mismatch between his or her conception of teaching and the more ideal practices being offered by a preparation program. To create disequilibrium, teacher educators plan the *optimum mismatch* between the student's ideas about teaching and the college- and field-based instructional activities (see Bolin, 1988; Glickman & Gordon, 1987), leading prospective teachers to (2) accommodation of new ideas and practices and, thus, to (3) acquiring a new level of equilibrium in which practice is based on preparation for the future rather than experiences of the past.

Creating a taxonomy of teacher development is a sensible approach *if* the significance of teacher beliefs is to be found in their role as cognitive barriers to new learning. However, the rational and objective aspects are only a small part of an individual's prior beliefs. Most beliefs are made up of the many more disorganized, ambiguous, and subjective elements that characterize life and learning and that defy reduction to a clean-cut set of stages. Nor can we discount the role of the knowing, choosing, acting individual who, though profoundly shaped and influenced by past experience (a developmental history), has the capacity to be self-critical and interpret his or her own experiences and traditions. Hence, moving too quickly from research about the thematic material of teacher belief systems to a cognitive ordering of them or to prescriptions for practice would be a mistake, however welcome stages of development and accompanying standards of practice might be to teacher educators.

Making Sense of Experience

If one accepts Dewey's notion that education is the continuous reconstruction of experience, it seems reasonable to suppose that experience must
be *examined* in order for meaningful reconstruction of it to take place. But
experience is not a tidy concept. It must be seen as the sum of an individual's
history, including actual events, fictionalized events, and interpretations
placed on them when they happened and as they are remembered. Experience is far more chaotic and contradictory than orderly and seamless. It
is shaped by the social and cultural context in which events occur as well
as the events themselves. Yet much of the research on teacher beliefs has
proceeded as if the teacher's personal knowledge were cognitive in nature
and culturally neutral.

More important than how teacher educators interpret personal
knowledge is how teachers themselves understand and make sense of
prior conceptions and beliefs. We need to know how people interpret
their experiences if we are to help them to meaningfully reconstruct it in
light of knowledge about teaching and learning. And we need to know
more about the nature of personal knowledge if we are to help teachers
honor the personal knowledge of their students and other teachers rather
than buying into the social, cultural, and racial hegemony around them.
In looking at Kay's early recollection of a positive school experience, along
with recollections of other teachers (pre- and inservice), we consider how
she and they interpret experience. Their early recollections are seen not
as realities but as highly significant "remembrances" that suggest what
is important to them in the present.

CROSS-CULTURAL EARLY RECOLLECTIONS OF SCHOOL

Overlapping with my experience as a teacher educator and researcher
working with preservice students in the United States have been experiences teaching teachers in Japan and China. Over the years, I have heard
countless early recollections of school, and I have been struck with how
similar they seem to be—Kay's early memory is not unlike the recollections of other teachers in other places in the world.

Recollections relating to basic human needs—such as health, safety,
belonging, being loved and esteemed, and desire for self-fulfillment—
harken back to Abraham Maslow's (1968) hierarchy of needs. Many stretch
across cultural boundaries, but if knowledge is socially and culturally
influenced, it stands to reason that in taking a closer look at Kay's *personal*
knowledge, there might be important, subtle cultural differences. If so,

we can question whether it is possible to understand Kay's personal knowledge without probing these differences. Recollections of my students across national boundaries (from 23 U.S., 22 Chinese, 18 Japanese, and 17 expatriate teachers living in Japan) offer considerable insight into the personal knowledge of teachers and underscore the significance of cultural sensitivity in teaching, whether in the school or college classroom. Looking at cross-cultural recollections seems to lead us away from Kay but, in the end, allows us to return to her at a deeper level and think beyond her experience to the broader world of teacher education.

Similarity in Themes

When Kay tells about her early positive recollection, she uses the words *excited, fabulous, happy*, and *singled out*. Teachers in China and Japan (including a group of expatriates whom I refer to as Internationals) use similar words, such as *encouraged, happy, excited, proud, loved*, and *recognized* in describing positive recollections. Words such as *embarrassing, humiliated, terrible, depressed*, and *hated* pepper the negative recollections. Just as the first core session in which students discuss early school memories is characterized by animation, so are the classrooms in Tokyo and Nanjing. As teachers share recollections with each other, there are outbursts of laughter, smiling, and a kind of joyfulness that is hard to describe but permeates the classroom in response to positive images. Frowning, expressions of outrage or sympathy—such as "Oh no!" or even pounding the table—characterizes discussions of negative images. Almost all of the teachers in Nanjing, who spoke English in class, immediately revert to Chinese, with their facial expressions and the rapidity of exchange illustrating their involvement. (Groups in Tokyo had some expatriates who did not speak Japanese, so their exchange is usually in English.)

All the teachers talk about memories of a *relationship with or special notice from a teacher*, a particular *honor or achievement*, an extraordinary moment or *special event, friendship and camaraderie*, and a special *responsibility or leadership* activity. Although the recollections share these themes, there are differences, as the memories are examined more closely and compared by group.

Differences in Agency

Clues to differences among Chinese, International, Japanese, and U.S. teachers may be teased out by looking at the "movement" within a recollection. Movements involve key actors and actions that are part of recollections and suggest agency—who or what is acting or acted upon. Movement may be related to *teacher agency, self-agency, group agency, or circumstances.*

1. *Teacher agency* is the result of teacher initiation or focus on the teacher. The teacher is acting upon the student; for example, "Each class in our school performed in a day-long show held for parents and members of the community. Each student could participate in an activity—dance, a play, group song, etc. My teacher felt I could perform on the trapeze, swinging above a thick mat" (Rob, U.S.). The movement in this recollection of a teacher's special notice is in the teacher acting on Rob by recognizing his talents.
2. *Self-agency* involves initiative and/or focus on self. Dehong (China) recalls an assignment to memorize a passage about the Great October Revolution in Russia. "Nobody in my class could recite it without making any mistake, but I could. The teacher singled me out for praising. I felt very proud of it. From that time on, I am determined to be one of the best students in my class." Special notice comes from the teacher because Dehong recited without a mistake. Focus is on her feelings of accomplishment, pride, and resolve.
3. *Group agency* involves classmates or significant others such as family. Yoshie (Japan) recalls, "On sports day, which is called *Undo-kai* in Japanese, fifth- and sixth-graders did a folk dance, in which a boy and a girl dance hand in hand. I remember we were a little bit shy with each other, but it sure was an exciting occasion for us." In Yoshie's recollection of a special event, emphasis is on the fun and camaraderie of the group. This is similar to Kay's early recollection. Like Yoshie, Kay recalls the excitement of a special event—learning to read—but emphasis is on being at the table with the group.
4. *Circumstance* is a situation or force that does not involve direct initiative by the teacher, self, classmates, or family. Lorraine (International, Euro-Japanese) remembers a special relationship with a teacher at an international school in Korea and is taken with the unusual circumstance. She learns that her teacher's father had taught her father when he was a child in another country. "Miss G's conversations with my father reminiscing about their school days made me aware that my father was also a child at one time in life with a lot of questions in life and that he was not only that authoritative figure whom I saw at home."

Most recollections of school, regardless of their theme, involve teacher agency. But while teacher agency characterizes movement in most Japanese teachers' recollections, *none* of their recollections have to do with teacher relationship or special notice. Here cultural nuances become very important.

Keiko Sawaguchi, a Japanese preservice teacher studying in the United States, is one of two Japanese teachers who looked at teacher recollections with me. She explains that Japanese children would not wish or expect special attention from the teacher. On the contrary:

> As a student, you have to do what everybody does in order to keep harmony or to pursue class learning goals. You had better not stick out because it might cause breaking harmony and the learning pace of the class. The teacher assumes that the student understands (so that the class can learn further). [For example], if I'm an elementary school child and math is not my favorite subject or is hard for me to understand, even though I don't understand, I won't say so. Even if some of the classmates feel the same way, they do not express their questions and struggle; therefore, it appears that everybody understands the teacher. In addition, teaching is considered a high-status job position by Japanese society. Even though Japanese students may not always understand the teacher, it is hard for them to express their thoughts sometimes because they are intimidated by the teacher's high status.

Group agency, present in the largest number of Japanese recollections, seems consistent with the cultural norm of the group taking precedence over the individual.

Teacher memories fall into somewhat predictable themes that are similar across cultural boundaries. By looking at agency, or who does the acting and who is acted upon, subtle cultural nuances suggest how different values may be lie beneath similar memories.

COMPARING THEMES IN POSITIVE RECOLLECTIONS

Kay's early recollection takes on more meaning when it is placed in the context of a social, cultural milieu and contrasted with other milieus. Differences in the meanings associated with experiences related to the themes of teacher relationship or special notice, honor or achievement, and the like are apparent among individuals within the same cultural context and more so when compared across cultures. As we look at positive recollections of other teachers around each of these themes and consider agency, Kay's recollection will also be examined.

A Teacher Relationship or Special Notice

Recollections within the theme of *a teacher relationship or special notice* included receiving special praise, a teacher's act of kindness, or an intellectually inspiring teacher. Roughly a third of all recollections involved a teacher relationship or special notice and teacher agency. It is possible, however, to enjoy a teacher's attention because of one's own agency, as we saw in Dehong's recollection.

Special notice from the teacher is seen as rescue from an unpleasant situation, in Min's recollection (U.S.):

> I am Korean and I came to the U.S. when I was 9 years old. I didn't speak a word of English, and I was horrified. I hated school. I cried nearly every day. However, my teacher helped me learn English. She stayed with me after school and at recess.

Kindness from a teacher is also apparent in Jun's description (China):

> We had a teacher who came from a teacher's college, and he was in his probation. One time I got my hands dirty after playing with other classmates. The young student teacher saw my hands, took me to his office, and washed them. It made me moved and impressed to a deep extent.

Wenwei (China) recalls how a teacher built on her experiences and helped her to feel competent and included:

> I often moved from one place to another when I was young. When my teacher knew my moving experience, she asked me to tell the whole class: what I saw, what I heard, and what friends I made during the traveling. I made such a successful demonstration that my teacher suggested my writing a composition for competition. As a result I got first prize. I was so happy, and I won respect from friends.

Given the young age at which children enter school and the prominence of teachers in school experiences, it seems reasonable that the most significant aspect of early schooling is how one relates to and is treated by the teacher. However, if children are socialized to see themselves as part of a group rather than individually, teacher relationship may not be as significant as experiences and activities that promote the group, as

Keiko noted earlier in explaining the total absence of recollections of teacher relationship by Japanese teachers. Tetsuto (Japan) explains his recollection in relation to the group in Japanese culture by quoting the proverb, "The nail that sticks up shall be hammered down."

This is in marked contrast to the Chinese teachers—for half of them, recollection was of teacher relationship. I discussed Chinese teachers' reflections with Xiaoman Zhu, a professor at Nanjing Normal University. She sees them as consistent with the way teachers are viewed in Chinese society. The teacher is a trusted friend, one who comes right after family in traditional Chinese philosophy, with Heaven and the Emperor preceeding.

Recollections of teacher relationships and special notice are complex. As adults, the teachers realize that their current opinions and beliefs may challenge their childhood interpretations. This is apparent in Kay's early memory. She recalls the excitement of being chosen to be at the table with the group reading "Dick and Jane." But as an adult, she describes the situation as "bizarre" because not everyone got the same opportunity. This contradiction between child and adult knowledge is also apparent in Liping's memory (China) of teacher notice. She sees that sometimes positive notice to one student has negative consequences for others:

> When I was studying in my primary school, I was especially competent at maths. I could work out any question the teacher raised in class, even though some of them were difficult. Therefore, my maths teacher liked me very much. Once a boy fell asleep in maths class and the teacher got very angry. He woke the boy up and said, "You have no right to sleep in my class. If Zhou Liping fell asleep, I would stop my teaching in case I would make noise." On hearing those words, I felt happiest. I thought it was a kind of acknowledgment.

Even though it was a happy experience for her, Liping goes on to say, "Now I am also a teacher. When I recall this experience, I don't feel happy. Instead I feel a bit of sympathy with the boy. Maybe these words hurt the boy greatly." Liping finds it difficult to reconcile her child perception of an experience with her adult knowledge. Early recollections are important in communicating feelings about events and impressions of these events, but they are not as reliable in telling us the exact details of events. As we have seen, a child's interpretation of experience may be contrary to adult understanding of the experience. One of the complexities of personal knowledge is that it is ambiguous and contradictory.

An Honor or Achievement

When teachers wrote about an honor or achievement as distinct from special notice or recognition from the teacher, their focus was on the thrill, excitement, and satisfaction of the achievement. In most instances, the satisfaction seems to be in the accomplishment and an internal sense of honor more than in outward recognition itself, though public recognition is clearly part of the remembered experience. About a quarter of all teachers recalled experiences such as winning a prize for academic success or some other skill, a personal success that was its own reward, being recognized or honored in a special way, and defying the expectation of others.

As we saw earlier, in Kay's recollection of being chosen to be part of a reading group, and Liping's notice from the teacher, the joy of a childhood recollection is sometimes censored by the adult recalling. This is also apparent as Jodi (International, Australian) remembers being honored for a birthday:

> One of my happiest memories from first grade was having my birthday celebrated in class. We had a cake made from an empty ice cream container, and the teacher lit the candles and I blew them out. Actually, I had lied about the date of my birthday. My birthday had passed, but as someone else was celebrating their birthday on this particular day, I wanted to celebrate, too. (My birthday had been spent in another school in a different state, but it wasn't celebrated with the class). I felt very special when the class sang "Happy Birthday" to me and I got to blow out the candles. I felt bad, however, as it wasn't really my birthday.

In her child memory, the celebration outweighs cost in guilt. However, as an adult, Jodie recognizes that she achieved recognition under false pretenses. The power the experience still has for her suggests the importance young children attach to being celebrated. One cannot help but wish that the teacher had helped bridge the experience for Jodie by pointing out that the class had not been able to celebrate her birthday before. Whatever the teacher may have done or understood in celebrating Jodie's birthday is not a part of her recollection; the joy of being celebrated resides with her guilt.

Rick (U.S.) recalls having achieved the nearly impossible. "I was in gym class, standing at the half-court line, and I threw a basketball backwards, and it went into the basket. This happened [in front of] my gym teacher and some of the 'cool' kids. I felt a sense of glory."

Along similar lines, Hiromi (Japan) recalls defying the expectation of her dance teacher. Her recollection illustrates how what begins as a negative experience can be turned into a moment of triumph, a current running through several of the recollections:

> When I was 3 years old, I took Japanese dancing lesson. The instructor always scold at me, hit my legs or hands. One day, I went to the house for older people to perform dancing. There was a big stage in front of many older people. Many of them praised me with the words, "Wa, oh. How good this little girl is!" or "How cute this little girl is!" I remember the words they said clearly. Because it's my first time to be praised by many people.

The very early age at which this experience happened to Hiromi underscores its deep significance.

A Special Project or Event

Kay's early recollection is about a special event: learning to read in kindergarten. School plays, reading to the class, field trips, class projects, moments of awe or wonder, and the like were recalled by many of the teachers. For Japanese teachers, this was the most frequent subject of recollections. While many of the U.S. teachers also spoke of special events such as performances, the emphasis was on having been recognized by the teacher or on the achievement in winning a role rather than on the project itself.

Japanese teachers talked about activities as varied as getting to take a hamster home over a holiday, school festivals, and performances. Sakae remembers a moment of wonderment when a retired teacher took the class outdoors:

> That day, an older teacher (he was about my grandfather's age) took us to the woods. He talked about grass, weeds, insects, and birds in the woods. And then he took a box [a nest] from the tree and opened the top. There we saw some tiny eggs and some hatches. He said, "They are very delicate. You can't touch them, otherwise a mother bird won't come back to take care of them."
>
> It was the first time I experienced how birds live. He really made my eyes open to the nature. Since then, I've always loved and appreciated animals around us and the nature.

Maria (U.S.) remembers a moment of wonder when "it snowed in Fremont, California. I don't believe it has snowed there since that day in elementary school. It was just before Christmas, so it infused everything with magic."

Billy (U.S.), however, remembers a project: "In second grade, we read *Charlie and the Chocolate Factory*. After reading the book, we were instructed to build an invention that could be placed inside the factory. I built mine out of Legos. It was awesome. We shared our inventions with the class." For Xiaojun (China), getting to play outside was a significant memory. For Derrick (International, Jamaican), a field trip was most significant.

Teachers believe that they should support and nurture a sense of wonder and playfulness. Children should be able to use their creativity and have opportunities for special events. And teachers should take the pressure off students. Dengdi says that "some kids may need to be reached through what they love."

Jim (International, Euro-American), who has never forgotten the thrill of seeing his father at a play in which he had a part, urges that teachers "understand the importance of parents' involvement in a child's development at school as well as at home."

Recollections and teacher suggestions are reminders that special projects and events break into routine experience, making them more precious and memorable. It is also likely that multiple meanings are associated with early experiences. Some of the recollections of special projects will reflect expectations of the teacher, and others may relate to the joy of the event itself.

Additional Themes

Almost a quarter of the recollections did not quite fit into the major themes. Some teachers recalled friendship or camaraderie, being with a special friend, a friend intervening in a difficult situation, or being with play groups. A special responsibility or leadership was the subject of other recollections—for example, helping design the school playground, being class monitor, and arranging desks to suit the class. Recommendations that these teachers made emphasize the importance for children of friendship, leadership, and responsibility.

CONCLUSION

Teachers have powerful images of school that are based on their experiences. Early recollections of school reveal basic impressions about what school is, who teachers are and what they do, and the role of students. Most of the recollections reported here are about relationships with teachers that were encouraging or satisfying, honors and achievements that brought pride to the individual or his or her family, and special projects or events that were fun, enriching, or astonishing. These images persist over time, may be recalled with vividness, and have implications for practice. And, while they share common characteristics, recollections and teachers' interpretations of them are culturally situated. All of these differences suggest fruitful avenues for investigation of how teachers are formed.

Teachers have straightforward recommendations about teacher relationship. Teachers should rescue, act with kindness, broaden intellectual horizons, and help students feel competent and that they belong. *Encouragement* is a term frequently used in all of the recommendations for teachers. It appears across all themes and cultural groups.

Teachers have a variety of suggestions about how their early positive experiences should inform teacher practice. In the order of their prominence, they believe teachers should do the following:

- Support and build on student talents and strengths
- Be kind, respectful of students, and caring
- Encourage and/or praise students
- Recognize that learning includes more than academic subjects
- Recognize the student's active role in learning
- Step outside the routine and everyday to provide memorable experiences
- Be aware of the significance of their actions in the lives of students
- Recognize the significance of student friendships

To help teachers deconstruct personal knowledge is a valuable activity. In Kay's preservice experience, exercises designed to help her confront personal knowledge were probably helpful. But deconstruction alone does not mean that teachers understand what memories children will gather from school or the ways in which they interpret experience. Their experiences will be based, at least in part, on biography and culture. Because something was important to the teacher as a child does not mean it will be equally important to other children. In fact, it is no stretch of the imagination to suppose that a U.S. teacher who, with the best of intentions, singled out a newly arrived Japanese student for special attention could be acting in an insensitive manner, according to Japanese cultural norms.

So far, we have looked at positive recollections of school, beginning with Kay's early positive memory. Some of our most powerful and haunting memories are of aversive or negative experiences, however. Many teacher beliefs about teaching, children, schools, and learning are constructed from painful events. In the next chapter we look at Kay's early negative memory of school, again considering it alongside recollections of other teachers. Then, in remaining chapters we will see how Kay's personal knowledge comes into play in her continuing development as a teacher.

ઙ 3 ભ

Exploring Negative Personal Knowledge

> I just remember getting in trouble as a kid. I would just be
> mortified because I would get in trouble for talking or what-
> ever. I can specifically remember times.
> —Kay, May 2000

IN CHAPTER 2, we began to look at how Kay and other teachers construct personal meaning from the countless experiences they have had as children in schools. The earliest recollection one offers about schooling provides a condensed, or summary, statement about what has been significant in an individual's personal search for meaning. As we have been reminded by the literature on teacher personal knowledge, prior experiences of schooling and memories of these experiences have a profound impact on the ways in which a teacher draws meaning from preparation for teaching and life as a teacher. Rather than encountering personal knowledge as a problem to be overcome, examining these images suggests that they may be seen as creative and constructive sources of what is considered to be of ultimate value and the motivation to teach.

In this chapter, we begin to examine recollections of negative experiences. As we do so, we encounter powerful emotional material that describes frustration and embarrassment at best and, at worst, anguish, pain, and suffering.

KAY'S EARLY NEGATIVE RECOLLECTION

For Kay, like many teachers, negative experiences come to mind more quickly than positive ones. "I have a couple of negative ones," she quips, recalling embarrassment at "getting in trouble as a kid." She describes the most prominent:

> One time—it was kindergarten, and we were all milling about. I
> got into an argument with somebody over a piece of paper. I re-

member getting yelled at over that. The two of us were pulling at the paper, and I remember getting really yelled at. I don't know if I had to stand in the corner or just got put away from the group or something like that. I was 6, and I can totally remember that. I think that I didn't get into trouble all that often, so I remember. I think also because I felt wronged. I felt like it wasn't my fault. I felt like it was the other kid pulling the paper away, and I got in trouble for it. I remember feeling that it was unjust, and I remember not wanting to be separated from the rest of the kids. They *could tell* I was in trouble because I was pulled out! And I didn't want to be in trouble. I don't know if at that time I was afraid that my parents would find out, but in later school years that was always the issue that overlaid any getting in trouble—thinking my parents would find out.

A theme that we encounter repeatedly in Kay's reflections on her own development as a teacher is that of justice. She wants things to be fair. We recall that her sense of fairness clouds Kay's positive recollection because she understands the implicit injustice in singling out a group of students as "ready to read" and giving them special privileges. "That is bizaar in retrospect!" she laughs, shaking her head. But, at the time, "I was really happy to be the one who was singled out."

Now, as an adult, Kay sees the contradiction between the teacher's means and ends in both experiences. In the positive memory, the teacher enabled a group of students to feel good at the expense of others, who were likely to have felt diminished because they were not chosen. In the negative experience, the teacher apparently intended to punish but stirred a deep sense of outrage rather than repentance. As Kay points out:

If you're highlighting the one that is in trouble, that is just making them feel really bad. I think that was the biggest thing, since I was removed people were looking at me and I was obviously the kid in trouble. And it wasn't my fault. I didn't think it was my fault. But now as the teacher . . . half the time you have no idea whose fault it was: Two kids are pulling a paper, you are going to talk to both of them.

Earlier, we saw how adult understanding tempers early recollections. Kay understands her reading experience and the fight over the paper in an adult way. But, like Jodie and Liping, who have positive memories of a birthday and being commended at another child's expense, adult understanding does not erase the emotional impact of the event.

Kay has a visceral reaction as she describes her negative recollection. She physically moves into the story, readjusting her position from leaning back in a chair to forcefully leaning forward at the table—as if by being at the table in the moment connects her to her positive memory of being included and helps her to cope with the negative recollection. Perhaps it is an unconscious metaphor. Having described the situation, she pauses for a moment, recalling how she felt then, and now as a teacher—how it is nearly impossible to know who is at fault in so many disputes or to realize how things you intend for good can be experienced as negative by other children. "I think about that, even in the reading thing." Kay recognizes that while she may feel guilty about being singled out to learn to read, her teacher's intentions were probably not to exclude, but to build on the strengths of a group of precocious students.

This look into how Kay balances past and present realities is the stuff of which teacher deliberation is made. She consciously juxtaposes past experience with the present. This enables her to critique her own ideas about teaching and learning. We will revisit this process again and again as we follow Kay's evolution as a teacher.

Unjust treatment, the theme of Kay's recollection, is not an uncommon subject of teacher recollections. *Being humiliated and diminished* along with *unjust treatment* account for more than half the negative recollections of the teachers I spoke with. In fact, injustice and humiliation are often intertwining themes, with the prominence of one or the other varying from recollection to recollection. *Relationships with peers, being forced to do something*, and a *bad classroom environment* are other themes of recollections. Kay's recollection is punctuated by the words *wronged, unjust, in trouble*. The array of descriptive language used coveys the emotional nature of the material being described. *Alone, guilty, inferior, confused, scared, betrayed, judged, isolated, hurt, shocked, disgusted, ridiculed, crushed,* and *stupid* are words expressing some of the feelings associated with negative memories.

We will examine negative teacher recollections, comparing them to Kay's memory of the fight over paper, then speculate on the importance of a deeper understanding of personal knowledge in supporting the emotional life of both the classroom and the teacher. We will see how Kay's career is still full of impressions formed in her early encounters with school and how these impressions have been reconstructed in ways that have allowed her to utilize her teacher preparation and grow beyond it.

AGENCY IN EARLY NEGATIVE RECOLLECTIONS OF SCHOOL

In examining positive recollections, agency is critical in understanding cultural nuances. Agency involves whether an individual is the actor or is being acted upon in an experience. For the majority of teachers I spoke with—including Kay—the negative experience recalled was the result of teacher agency. The agency of circumstances is usually responsible when the experience is not the result of teacher actions. For example, Fanxia (China) remembers when the school building collapsed and students were buried under the rubble. Two students were killed. "We all cried. I was so lucky that I was saved, but I had serious injuries on my head. . . . I can remember the terrible scene." This was a traumatic experience that overshadowed every other recollection. But circumstances are not always tragic, even if they are humiliating at the time. Yasuko (Japan) remembers:

> There was a recorder presentation in music class when I was in fourth grade. I practiced a lot, and I had confidence to play the recorder. When I was waiting for my turn in front of the class, I felt something. I realized the rubber string of my knitted underpants was cut. I was [in] panic. I didn't want to show my miserable condition to my classmates. I had to keep my underpants up but at the same time I had to play the recorder. It was very hard to do them together. But fortunately, I managed to do it. My presentation was awful.

Group agency accounts for all of the early recollections that involved peer relationships. Michele (International, Euro-Canadian) remembers how the group made her feel like an outsider. A girl in her class began making fun of her because she left school early to go to ballet class. "She was calling me names and saying I was a goody-goody, and we got in a fight on the playground. All the kids gathered around and encouraged the fight. I felt very alone and isolated from the other kids."

Regardless of theme or cultural group, there were very few instances in which a situation seemed to be the result of an individual's own actions, or self-agency. It may be that children are generally so young and vulnerable at the time these experiences occur that they feel acted upon and powerless in the face of oppressive, frightening forces. Perhaps they do not see their own role in events, or, as Bettleheim (1987) observes, "the child is always convinced that his cause is just" (p. 97).

XiaoLi's (China) memory is an exception. She remembers a quarrel with her benchmate "who was very beautiful, with rosy cheeks, snow-white teeth, and bright black eyes. . . . I pushed her and she fell down on the ground with one of her teeth knocked out. She was [so] very sad and unhappy that she was absent from class for a week. I felt really sorry." In this case, the teacher did not blame XiaoLi but insisted that the girls apologize and called their attention to how they should be spending their time in class. But XiaoLi feels responsible, blaming herself.

One might suppose that because Japanese children are socialized to expect teachers to relate to the group more than to individuals, more of their negative recollections would be about being singled out by their teacher. However, being singled out in a negative way is an unpleasant memory for several teachers across cultural boundaries. What creates unpleasant and fearful memories for children is related to how they perceive an experience, whether it threatens their feeling of safety and well-being, and how it connects to their sense of what is right and just and to their sense of belonging and being valued as human beings. Being singled out for reprimand, as the target of teacher sarcasm, or in ways that highlight a child's inadequacies amounts to an assault on the child's sense of self and other in the world, however self and other have been culturally shaped.

COMPARING THEMES IN NEGATIVE RECOLLECTIONS

Differences in meaning associated with experiences that are seen as positive connect directly to how teachers are culturally perceived, their expected role, and what children expect of school. Differences in meaning associated with negative experiences are much more difficult to tease out and, at least on the face of things, seem less culturally specific, though we can speculate that there are profound differences once we are past the face of things. The broad themes of feeling humiliated or diminished, being unjustly treated, having negative relationships with peers, being forced to do something, and a bad environment in the classroom resonate across groups.

Being Humiliated or Diminished

Experiences that humiliate often make students feel like a failure, inferior, or ashamed. The fact that most of the humiliating or diminishing experiences were the result of teacher agency is a potent reminder of the power over students that teachers hold.

In most instances, the memory still smarts because it publicized a situation. Ellen (U.S.) recalls that in kindergarten, "We had to ask to use the bathroom which was just next door. I was afraid to ask. I had an accident, which was a terrible memory." She was humiliated. Other teachers recall being shamed in front of the class for not knowing something the teacher thought they should know. Dengdi (China) had to keep standing in front of the class when he couldn't answer a question, while Liew

(International, Malaysia) had to stand in the corner. But Liping (China) was shamed when her teacher ignored her:

> Once I was asked to answer a question. As I knew nothing about it, I kept silent. However, the teacher didn't criticize me. Instead, he asked another girl to answer it. . . . Her fluent answer earned her loud applause from classmates. I was ashamed to death. I hated the teacher. If he had criticized me, I wouldn't have minded.

Failing to pass an exam was a source of embarrassment, guilt, and loss of dignity for Pun, Dehong, and XiaoJun. MaJong felt inferior when "the teacher asked every student to turn in five fen and then took them to the cinema. As I was the only student who did not have any pocket money, I had to go home." Being excluded from the group is a negative memory for several teachers, but in MaJong's experience, the hurt and embarrassment are from having his situation become public.

Sometimes an embarrassing experience creates an aversion to activities, as it did for Christopher (International, Euro-American). He remembers being unable to tie his shoes as a kindergartner:

> I remember having to change from shoes to sneakers for our gym class. I remember that I was mortified the first time because I couldn't even tie my laces properly! I tied them half way and then tucked the strings into the sides of my sneakers. Then when we started to play, one of my sneakers slipped off. The teacher quickly called my attention to it in front of everyone . . . he told me to go out into the hall and come back when I had my shoes tied properly. Of course, I couldn't tie them myself, so I sat in the hallway crying for awhile. Then, finally [I] went to the nurse, and she was kind in helping me. Since then, I remember detesting PE class! I was so humiliated!

Billy (U.S.) recalls drawing animals in cages after a trip to the zoo. "I showed it to my teacher, and she told me I had done it wrong. She said the way I had arranged the animals wasn't accurate." Ali (U.S.) recalls "being singled out as being a hyperactive and problematic child."

Hiroshi (Japan) remembers when her first-grade Japanese teacher "read my composition in front of the class and pointed out that my Japanese . . . was very strange. He corrected my composition. I was very embarrassed." Ed (International, Euro-American) remembers that at his school boys were supposed to play on the grass and girls on the asphalt:

Well, everyone knows that super balls bounce better on hard ground. I went to play or bounce the ball on the side of the school on the asphalt, got "caught" committing such an ungodly crime, and was forced to stand in the hallway in front of the principal's office. . . . I was ashamed . . . and all the teachers expressed their surprise and shock at seeing me in the hall. I felt like the Hunchback of Notre Dame.

Sometimes trying to do something good is misunderstood and turns what might have been a positive experience into one that is confusing and embarrassing. Joe (International, Euro-American) tried to help another child in kindergarten by showing him the answer to a question. "The teacher got very angry with me, and I can still hear her shouting, 'Do your own work!' . . . I felt terrible after the teacher scolded me in front of the other students." Lorraine (International, Euro-Japanese) also remembers being scolded in front of everyone by her first-grade teacher. Lorraine had lied about finishing her milk at lunch, and when her teacher discovered milk leaking from her lunch pail, she was severely reprimanded. "To this day I shall never forget that moment." The lesson Lorraine learned was not about telling the truth, but about how crushing to the spirit a teacher can be.

Teacher sarcasm is the subject of Wenwei's recollection. It is in contrast to her positive memory, mentioned in Chapter 2, in which a teacher had her contribute expertise based on the fact that she had moved a number of times:

One day the teacher asked a question: "Where is the revolutionary birthplace?" Many pupils gave the wrong answer. I knew the answer, but I was so nervous and shy that I made a mistake. He looked at me, with an ironic expression on his face. "You come from a big city. But you don't know the answer. What a shame!" I was so shamed, my feelings were hurt, and I didn't want to go to that school anymore.

Hiroshi's recollection evoked feelings of betrayal. He had left his school bag and failed to notice until his teacher called and brought it for him. What was undoubtedly intended as a kindly act by the teacher went sour for Hiromi:

The next day, my PE teacher, who probably heard that story from my classroom teacher, talked about me during the PE class. Since PE was my favorite class and my mistake had nothing to do with PE, I was totally embarrassed and felt humiliated, insulted by my

PE teacher and also my classroom teacher who talked about it behind me.

So far, all of these memories of being humiliated involve teacher
agency. But for Shi (China), it was not being able to afford the school
tuition that brought embarrassment. In his recollection the emphasis is
on the situation itself, whereas in MaJong's memory it is the fact that
attention was called to his situation. Hua blamed herself (self-agency) for
letting her mind wander and the shame she felt as a result of being called
on and not knowing what the class was doing. Jolene (U.S.) remembers
being chosen last for teams in gym, "regardless of the sport. I suppose it
became a stigma—she's no good at gym. I was singled out in a negative
way." In her recollection the group's action is to blame.

Being shamed or humiliated leads to feelings of hurt, embarrassment,
anger, and hatred. Not only are the memories of being shamed unforgetta-
ble, but so are the feelings that occurred in the moment. Teachers were
astonished to find themselves blushing, feeling anger and frustration
again as they shared their memories with each other. They also noted
that the reactions of other teachers, who expressed outrage and sympathy
on hearing their stories, were comforting.

Unjust Treatment

Kay's recollection is about unjust treatment. She still smarts over the unfairness of being punished for a fight she did not start, even though, as an
adult, she recognizes that teachers cannot possibly know everything that
goes on in the classroom. Teacher injustice, from the perspective of children,
takes many forms. Zoya (U.S.) recalls, "My teacher called me to the front
of the room after we had turned in our book reports. I thought she was
going to praise me, but instead she told everyone what a cheater I was.
She said no one could have done such a good report." Injustice and humiliation go hand in hand in her recollection, as they do for Lina (Japan), who
recalls that she was the only one who admitted to the teacher that she had
forgotten to memorize an assigned passage for homework. It turned out
that a number of other students had also forgotten, but the teacher and
other students helped them along in saying something. "At the end the
teacher told us what grades we got individually. I was the only one who
got a C, and the others (including the ones who didn't do their homework
but recited anyways) got A or B. It was a very embarrassing experience."

The injustice of having done something good and being treated as
if he had done something bad still stings in Xiaoping's (China) memory,
much as a similar memory (helping a classmate) has stayed with Joe:

> One day on my way to school I found a wallet lying on the ground. I picked it up and tried hard to find its owner. But I failed. At last I just turned it in to a policeman. When I hurriedly got to the school, the class had already begun. I was severely scolded by my teacher. Oh my god, unfair! I did something good. But in return I was scolded. I felt sad and disappointed.

Noriko (Japan) cringes as she recalls the unfairness and insensitivity of a second-grade teacher who would not let her go to the bathroom. "I endured it for a long time. Finally, maybe 15 minutes later, although my class teacher didn't finish his talking, I asked him to let me go there." The teacher was sarcastic and refused permission. "I was almost dead!"

Makoto remembers both the injustice and the humiliation of being hit on the cheek by a PE teacher because a girl had lied about his behavior. He stood in front of the class and took the punishment. "I couldn't make an excuse just because she was so scared." Nebuko remembers how a homeroom teacher blamed her for the failure of her group to come up with a tape recording to play on a school broadcast. Already "depressed and unhappy" because the other children did not want to be involved and would not cooperate, she was stunned when her teacher said, "This is *all* your fault, Nebuko." Then "all my classmates started to blame me . . . I just cried." Nebuko sketches a teardrop on her paper and a figure of hands to eyes crying.

Kevin (International, Australia) recalls how excited he was to be in the top reading group in first grade and to be able to read. When it was his turn to read in reading circle, he came to the word *quack* and read it the way he thought a duck would say it.

> The other kids laughed, and I believe the teacher saw the event as a breakdown of discipline, and I was scolded. I remember feeling bad—but also confused because I couldn't understand her anger. I also remember being moved to a lower group. It seems like she taught me not to trust my own knowledge.

The injustice of being reprimanded for something he was proud of and meant for good still lingers with Kevin. And the teacher's response, even today, seems out of proportion to him. A subtext in all of the memories of injustice from a teacher is *not being believed and respected.*

Experiences of injustice also create feelings of disappointment, disillusionment, hatred, humiliation, anger, resentment, and the desire for revenge. Barry (International, Euro-Canadian) remembers giving a boy who started a fight "an extra elbow as I passed him, which resulted in me getting extra punishment . . . I guess I couldn't resist righting some of the injustice of it." Like Kay, Barry felt that being punished for a fight he did not start was unfair.

Other Themes

More than half of the negative recollections, Kay's included, are about being humiliated, diminished, or treated unjustly. There were a few about other themes and a few that seemed to be unique unto themselves. *Relationships with peers*, *being forced to do something* that was distasteful or beyond the ability of the child, and what might best be described as a *bad classroom environment* make up the rest of the themes.

Relationships with Peers. In Kay's recollection, she is fighting. While this involves negative interaction with a classmate, the memory is about injustice. For other teachers, however, interactions with classmates are the subject of the memory. Eric remembers getting into "a fight with another boy for no other reason than that I was of Jewish background." Marc (International, Japanese-American) remembers being ridiculed by peers. "There was one time on the crowded school bus when I looked right in my sensi's eyes, stood on my toes to call her, and in a clear voice, called, 'Grandma!' All of the older kids started snickering, giggling, and even laughing out loud."

Julie (U.S.) recalls being teased about being Korean. Other students "pointed to their eyes and made fun of my slanted eyes." Anju remembers returning to the United States after 4 years in West Africa. "I felt like a real outsider in many ways." She recalls that she didn't have winter clothes. "One girl made me feel really weird because I was wearing a skirt."

Name-calling was hurtful to Shuxia (China). Children gave her a nickname that "made me feel shameful; I didn't want to go to school forever." A quarrel that led to the breakup of a friendship is the subject of ZhiDan's (China) memory.

> We were playing a game. I declared that she broke the rule and she denied it, when, in fact, she did wrong. After a while, she exclaimed that it was I who had made a mistake and that I failed. Undoubtedly I felt very indignant. And we were not good friends anymore.

But for Chikako (Japan), being ignored was the source of pain. "It was a kind of 'play' among students. One student said, I don't like her, and the other students followed and ignored me . . . I was very hurt."

Being Forced to Do Things. A small number of teachers across all groups recall being made to do things they did not like to do or did not feel qualified to do. These experiences ranged from freezing in front of the class when trying to recite (Donna, U.S.; Derrick, International) to being made to take part in sports events (Chunyan, China; Sake and Tiusako, Japan). All of these memories were related to teacher agency—the teacher was forcing the behavior.

Words such as *hated, sad, unpleasant, dislike, annoyed, frozen, ashamed, pressure,* and *stress* appear throughout. Derrick remembers that he did not go to school the day after he had forgotten lines for a part he was forced to memorize at the last minute.

A Bad Classroom Environment. While there were only a few teachers who recalled negative memories that reflected on a difficult classroom environment, they are worth noting. A teacher who explodes in front of children or is too strict (Dorothy, U.S.; Yoshi, Japan) creates a situation that is characterized by tension, worry, and fear. When teachers do not protect children, they can feel betrayed, as did Keikio (Japan) when her teacher failed to do anything about a bully. These memories underscore how important it is for the classroom to be a safe place—safe from adults and from other children. Teachers should not allow children to go too far or engage in behavior that is harmful to others. Rob (U.S.) recalls being bitten by another child. Teachers also recalled experiences in which they believed they were allowed to go too far, for example, ridiculing a child with physical disabilities and surrounding a boy in the restroom and urinating on him. In both instances, these teachers felt sharp pangs of guilt about their childhood behavior and believed that teachers should draw the line, protecting children from their worst inclinations.

CONCLUSION

Kay's unpleasant memory of school, like her positive memory, summarizes basic beliefs about teaching. She, like other teachers whose memories we have examined, recognizes the discrepancies between her child and adult standards for both student and teacher behavior. For the most part, their experiences remind teachers that they must recognize the child's perspective in assessing the consequences of intervention and provide sympathy and support when things go wrong. In some cases, teachers recognize that their own teachers were out of bounds. Their own painful experience has made them realize how crucial it is that children find a safe and trustworthy ally in the teacher.

Implications of recollections—both negative and positive—seem straightforward. Teachers need to be more caring. While it is unlikely that any teacher-preparation or staff development program would not agree, it is apparent that teacher education and development are driven by multiple, sometimes conflicting, necessities. It is necessary to prepare teachers to understand how children learn. It is necessary that they have sufficient grounding in a discipline or, in the case of elementary education programs, *disciplines* that contain the knowledge from which they will draw what is to be taught. It is necessary that they learn teaching methods suitable to their discipline(s), classroom management techniques, and the like and that they have periodic opportunities to update their knowledge and skills.

Beyond these basics is another set of necessities, however: understanding of curriculum development, social and political knowledge of schools, insight into how race and culture undergird all human knowing. When they understand curriculum development, teachers can make the curriculum suitable for the particular needs of children. Knowledge of the social and political realities of schools and how they work allows teachers to negotiate the complexities of school life for themselves and their students. Insight into how race and culture undergird all human relationships and knowing allows teachers to see below the surface of things and work for more just human interactions and structures in school.

Given these multiple demands on teacher-preparation programs, it is easy enough for teacher educators to take it for granted that teachers will be caring and bypass the *emotional life of teaching*. In the press to equip teachers with the technical knowledge and skills that will be required of them to be successful, it is easy to lose sight of the fact that who the teacher is *as a person* and chooses to become will influence what happens in the classroom. Teachers are left with little professional support for nourishing their own sense of being as knowing, thinking, acting, feeling, and striving individuals.

Yet understanding of the self as more than intellectual may be one of the most important requirements in learning to guide students. In his classic study of teachers, Arthur Jersild (1955) suggests that self-understanding "requires something quite different from the methods, study plans, and skills of a 'know-how' sort that are usually emphasized in education" (p. 3). Self-understanding is related to the individual's search for meaning, which is grounded in the dialectal relationship between one's cognitive, physical, emotional, aesthetic, spiritual, and social being.

There are teachers who make a decision to become a teacher because they want to be able to say, "Never again, never again will a child have to suffer what I suffered." Yet they are given little, if any, support in applying their own experiences to the process of learning about teaching. Learning to teach is also, perhaps even primarily, learning about self. Our own experiences of success and failure offer us the opportunity to enlarge our capacity for compassion that allows us to celebrate and mourn with students. Thomas Moore (1997) suggests that if such experiences are to help us to become more human, we must attend to them. He writes, "Modern psychology has manufactured a philosophy of light, with goals of adjustment, normalcy, mental hygiene, and correctness. But actual life demands a more inclusive worldview that honors the gaps and failures that bring both pain and humanity" (p. 241).

We might add that modern teacher preparation has focused on goals of learning how to teach, but actual life in the classroom "demands a more inclusive worldview that honors the gaps and failures that bring both pain and humanity." Because Kay's preparation program attempted to do this, however inadequately, her struggle to reconstruct prior experience in a personally and professionally meaningful way offers some insight into the importance of such struggles and of recognizing a larger worldview.

℘ 4 ℭ

The Persistence of Personal Knowledge

The students unfortunately do have to do some things they
don't want to, and if I don't do something when they say it's
boring, they will begin to declare things boring before they
give them a chance.

—Kay, 1989

KAY'S EARLY RECOLLECTION of a positive experience was about learning
to read in kindergarten. It was fun for her, something that made her
feel special and competent. Her recollection summarizes the belief into a
compressed, simple form. This belief, that learning should be fun, becomes
the source of a dramatic contradiction between her personal and growing
professional knowledge and, therefore, an opportunity for growth. In this
chapter, we look again at Kay's entry into teaching, focusing more intently
on personal knowledge. Kay first encounters a discrepancy and recognizes
it as such, then she begins to critique it, and finally she is able to accommodate discrepant views. A process of *reconstructing* her own thinking about
the place of fun in learning begins. It is a process that will continue
throughout Kay's career.

Kay's negative recollection of having been "wronged" also plays out
in what is important to her as a neophyte teacher. Reconstruction seems
to follow a slightly different path as she encounters issues of justice and
fairness in her first teaching experiences.

THE CONDITIONS FOR RECONSTRUCTION OF KNOWLEDGE

Janet, Kay's cooperating teacher, is a graduate of the TC preservice program and follows a constructivist approach to teaching. Initially, the first
semester student-teaching placement is a comfortable one for Kay. Janet's
creation of a classroom environment and use of materials confirm Kay's
undergraduate experience in Ithaca, where games and hands-on activities

were the only way to get children to come for academic tutoring. But her emergent theory about learning through interest and fun resides alongside as yet unarticulated notions of school as a place where she had fun following a traditional curriculum format—a format that is *not fun* for all children. What was fun for Kay as child is not consistent with Kay as an adult learning about new approaches to reading and literacy that go beyond grouping children homogeneously for reading in basal readers.

The contradiction bubbles under the surface when she begins to wonder about what actually constitutes fun for children, a reflection prompted by her encounter with whole language. She mentions this in her journal the first week of student teaching, describing a "great experience" with Violet, a first-grader who doesn't know how to write her name. Janet has suggested that Kay help Violet form letters in salt. "This worked really well because at first she was just fascinated with playing with the salt, so she was willing to practice the letters. After a while she was able to pick out each letter and write." Kay is intrigued by how whole language "works," commenting, "I'm definitely seeing how much harder it is to use such processes as writing process or whole language. The teacher has to be much more creative."

The ambiguity does not actually surface, however, until Kay is asked in a writing assignment for a core class to compare her own first-grade experience to that of her student-teaching classroom. She begins with the obvious, noting differences in room arrangement. In elementary school she experienced assigned seats and "singular desks," while "Janet never assigns seats." She observes that the seating pattern develops cooperative relationships and a form of independence from the teacher. She contrasts the curriculum, observing that in her student-teaching classroom "the curriculum is more hands-on and personal." She wonders if her own willingness to write might have been stunted by having to spell things correctly, and she expresses approval of invented spelling.

Recognizing Discrepancies

Kay is feeling that constructivist theory, although she has not named it, has some benefits that she did not experience. But the contradiction in her beliefs sharpens as she recalls that she *liked her more traditional experience* as a child:

> I remember math as being all workbooks and dittos. This causes rote memory instead of comprehension in many children, although I remember the feeling of achievement I felt when I finished a workbook or packet of dittos. I am not sure this will occur with

the more manipulative work, since there is not much of a finished product. Maybe there will be more of this in the future, or perhaps the students will feel accomplished because they really learned something.

Now the discrepancy is becoming conscious, and she will wrestle with it as the semester progresses. Each point at which she mentions the interest in whole language or other constructivist methods presents an opportunity for her supervisor to begin to build the kind of mental scaffold, or bridge, that will help her acquire more mature ways of thinking about her work (Bolin, 1988). While Kay and her supervisor may have discussed the points of ambiguity and potential conflict that occur in her journal, there are no supervisor comments that suggest this level of engagement. Kay is apparently only jarred into dealing with the inherent conflict and ambiguity within her nascent theory of teaching when she is asked to write a reflection paper for core on how she learned to read.

Kay recalls ability groups in reading at her school. She was a bright student and loved the feeling of competition. But she questions the effect of ability grouping on students' self-esteem, particularly those who are not in a "higher" group. She also remembers that she "loved any workbook work throughout the years. I felt like a real 'student' when I was doing workbooks." The conflict becomes more apparent to her as she writes:

> Everything I described goes very much against the whole-language concept currently held by many. Because of my parents' encouragement and help in the reading area, I was able to enjoy and do well in non-holistic language learning; however, I can clearly see that someone without my home background or relative ease with reading would do much better in a whole-language program than the reading programs of the past.

Kay has sought to resolve the contradiction by searching for an explanation that will account for the fact that an approach that was good for her is so counter to what she is learning about in methods courses at the college and what she sees happening in her student-teaching classroom. While the contradiction may never be fully resolved, Kay is aware of it.

Becoming Self-Critical

She has begun to critique and reconstruct her personal knowledge and is developing groundwork for questions about what knowledge is of most worth and for whom. In order to develop, sustain, and deepen this self-critique, most students need support. Given the paucity of supervisory comment in her dialogue journal, it is difficult to say whether or not her supervisor played a critical role in this process. Even so, writing the journal entries seems to prompt Kay to reflect. Her cooperating teacher provides a model of reflective practice, and core sessions and assignments are challenging Kay. Her faculty reader, who follows all of her work for the core, provides extensive feedback and raises critical questions, judging by comments made on her papers. She is also challenged by a small support group of student-teaching peers, led by a faculty member, which meets weekly to reflect on professional issues related to their immediate experiences.

Whether or not Kay resolves contradictions is not as important as the fact that she notices them. She may, in fact, come to realize that throughout her career she will have divided opinions about ways of teaching and learning. She may also realize that some impulses that are prompted by past experience are ones that she will choose not to act upon because they are not congruent with what she now believes.

SEPARATION OF THEORETICAL AND PRACTICAL KNOWLEDGE

As Dewey (1904) postulated, preparation programs that promote the development of teachers who are experimental about their work and inclined to be students of teaching are likely to leave their graduates at an initial disadvantage. Graduates will have fewer "good things to do" in the short run and may seem less successful than other beginning teachers. But the ability to study a situation and invent appropriate activities that are grounded in an understanding of children, subject matter, and pedagogy will lead to a stronger teacher over time. When teacher educators emphasize the kind of experimental attitude that integrates theoretical and practical knowledge, they often meet with resistance, however. As Dewey pointed out, students very much want to know a set of "how-tos." Compounding the difficulty is the fact that most schools expect student teachers to come with a repertoire of good things to do rather than with a repertoire of good questions.

Earlier, we saw how Kay reflects on the relation between theory and practice now that she is an experienced teacher. Arriving at her present understanding required that she struggle with her own preference for "how-tos" and her theoretical inclinations, or embryonic theories of teaching and learning. Britzman (1986) identified the tendency in her student teachers to prefer practical knowledge, describing it as the cultural myth that teachers are self-made. Closely akin to this idea, perhaps inherent in it, is the notion that teaching is something one does, not something one thinks about (Bolin, 1987). Reflection, when it occurs, is likely to be on actions and whether or not they "work" without any theoretical understanding. What works is usually related to what produces greater control and measurable learning results. Such utilitarian thinking emphasizes the practical, rather than the intricate dynamics related to why particular actions or activities work and whether or not they are appropriate.

Questioning Official Knowledge

Kay notes after her first day of student teaching, "I dealt with the students by instinct, and they responded positively right away." During her second week of student teaching, she writes of an activity that she has led: "I completely imitated how I've watched Janet do it in the past few days. I think a great deal of this year will be at least partial imitation. But I'll learn to conform her ways to fit me."

At the same time, she is working on an assignment for the core that is designed to promote careful integration of theory and practice, a semester-long child study using a variety of ethnographic techniques. She notes in her journal:

> I enjoyed doing the child study because you miss so much about a student when you have to watch 27 of them. From mine I discovered that Mike was not doing the group lessons with the group. When Janet would ask the class to do something like count, Mike would just sit there. Now Janet knows he needs a little extra encouragement. The books point out how essential this observation is and I agree, but if a teacher is by herself in the classroom, how would she ever have time to do it? Even with two of us there, we are both constantly involved in something.

In terms of her future as a deliberative teacher, this passage suggests some important beginnings. Kay is weighing what she has read about observation, as assigned in the core, and learning that there is value in doing the assignment. She is also questioning how realistic it is. The inclination to question the "official knowledge" of her textbooks and core can deteriorate into a dismissal of theoretical knowledge, or it can be encouraged as a way of moving toward deliberative knowledge, which examines the social and political nature of what is taught (Van Manen, 1977). Perhaps the difference will be determined by whether she is allowed to simply complain or is challenged to go deeper with her questioning.

Meanwhile, though Janet is a model of how one can integrate both theoretical and practical knowledge, Kay's broader field setting validates practical more than theoretical knowledge. Kay attended PDS meetings in which faculty challenged assignments such as the child study, arguing that too much valuable time in the classroom was wasted in doing "work for TC." PDS faculty constantly pushed for more time in classrooms and fewer university requirements that impinge on that time. For example, students are required to play an observer role during the first 2 weeks of student teaching and begin to collect data on the classroom and a child study subject. Teachers wanted them to immediately become fully immersed in the life of the classroom, primarily by taking on small groups. So, as is the case with most student teachers, Kay heard conflicting messages about what knowledge is most valuable in learning to teach. She was not immune to the tension.

Another assignment in which she is to look closely at a child who is particularly challenging to her (academically, socially, behaviorally) prompts Kay to consider the bridge between theory and practice and reflects her own struggle with what is worth doing. She observes:

> By doing my challenging child study on Violet, I am consciously seeking her out more often and am finding out some great stuff. Today during writing I conferenced with her, and I coaxed her into explaining her picture to me. . . . I really feel this observation could produce very beneficial results. I'll have to make sure that we follow up on what I come up with.
>
> It's nice to feel that one of the "pain in the ass" assignments is really worthwhile. I'm realizing that they probably are, but when I'm really pressed for time it's hard to keep this perspective.

Kay's interest in practical matters is reflected in another description of Janet. Janet has explained to her that she has not taught first-grade before and that they will be learning a great deal together. "I do not see this as a disadvantage. If anything, it will give me a chance to see how a teacher discovers what works and what does not." In her experience with the after-school program in Ithaca, she had felt herself fortunate to learn a number of methods from teachers, and she is eager to add to her collection.

Integrating Theoretical and Practical Knowledge

If Kay had been assigned to a cooperating teacher whose main focus was practical knowledge, she might have become less inclined to reflect on anything other than the technical aspects of teaching and learning. However, while Janet is interested in "what works," she approaches activities with an experimental attitude, thinking about why they are or are not effective and toward what ends. Perhaps more important is the fact that Janet supports program requirements by encouraging Kay in self-reflection, rather than subverting program requirements by replacing them with more "practical" activities and, in effect, devaluing self-reflection. For example, 5 weeks into the semester, Kay tries a lesson that includes a challenge of sex-role stereotyping. The children grasped the concept sooner than she had imagined they would and she finds herself out of material. Things fall apart. Janet encourages her to think about what went well and when the change in children's behavior occurred. "I admit I was convinced my lesson was a flop until Janet explained this to me. I think I can look and see what went wrong with my lessons but almost as important is seeing what went right, or if something didn't work, what worked better." In this instance, her supervisor also affirms an experimental attitude, in comments in the dialogue journal, noting that it is as important to understand what went well as what did not. "And, as we have discussed, thinking about why things work and don't provides much more depth to understanding the teaching learning process."

Six years later, in reflecting on the role that Janet played in her development as a teacher, Kay recalled:

> Janet definitely was going through stuff, you know, listening to people and trying to apply [their theories] in her classroom. I think she was always speaking about theories she'd heard. . . . Janet would definitely sit there and think through. . . . She wrestled with issues, was always "testing" things.

Kay remembered that as a student teacher, she saw this as nothing short of amazing. At the time, Kay wrote in her second reflection paper for Core:

> The ideas that I am hearing from Janet, the other teachers at [the school] and at Teachers College all sound amazing. A lot of these ideas are different from some of the past; however, some parts of first grade will never change. The children are getting their first taste of the importance of school, and it is a very emotional time for them. There is so much to learn during this year, as well as so much to teach. It is a challenging year for everyone involved.

By the end of her first semester, Kay has had numerous opportunities to surface, critique, and revise internal images about the relationship between theory and practice to accommodate her new learning. By mid-semester, she has become much more experimental in her work, accepting the need for careful planning but learning to act spontaneously. A learning episode is becoming an occasion for observing and learning about children. She incorporates what she has discovered in one lesson into her plans for the next day. Learning to think on her feet, become a careful observer of children, reflect on the experience, and utilize what she learns to plan for the future are ways in which the practical and more theoretical may be integrated. Integration is more likely if there is sufficient emphasis on why activities are appropriate as well as whether or not they worked. Janet strengthens this connection.

By the seventh week the two are able to collaboratively make decisions in the act of teaching, as well as reflect and plan together before or after the fact. Janet helps Kay to see how the activities they are doing are part of an integrated curriculum. Kay finds that this is fun for children and for herself as a teacher, which draws on a prior image of what education ought to be. The tensions between prior images, and growing understanding of teaching as theory in action, continue to be apparent, however, as we examine how she deals with the issue of social control, one of the barriers to reflective practice delineated in the literature.

SOCIAL CONTROL OF CLASSROOMS AND CHILDREN

One of the most discouraging findings in the research on teaching is the eroding effect of school culture on fledgling teachers who enter with the hope of doing good and soon become skilled in the authoritarian "pedagogy of poverty" (Haberman, 1991). The thought of being alone in the classroom and in charge is so overwhelming to most student teachers that it colors almost everything they do. Until they feel confident that they can control student behavior, issues of discipline preoccupy them. Kay is no exception. Her journal is peppered with references to the enormity of the task, in dealing with both individual children and a whole class.

Examining Control

Controlling the whole class is an issue from the beginning. Here we see how her ideas about control and inclinations to respond in particular ways are driven by the *teacher shoulds* described in Chapter 1. Describing an episode during her first week, she uses terms such as *felt at a loss, completely frustrated,* and *miserable* to describe how she felt when children refused to obey a request to walk quietly to the cafeteria. Implicit in the reaction is the belief that *teachers should* be in command and control. Janet helps her to examine the episode. "But I really have a gut feeling that I should have been able to do it. Part of me is saying, 'If I can't bring 10 kids up one flight quietly, how am I going to handle a classroom of 28 or so by myself?' Agh!!!"

She discusses the difficulty in getting children to quiet down, the fact that she feels uncomfortable using games and exercises that make her feel "stupid" in order to settle them down, and how "disheartened" she feels when lessons do not go smoothly. "My biggest problems are in classroom management. I do not know how to motivate the utterly unmotivated children. I know these two aspects are the hardest areas of teaching, but I want to know how to do it!!"

She also worries about controlling individuals and small groups. For example, during her third week in the classroom she attempts to teach a reading group and two of the children keep wandering off.

> I found myself getting very frustrated and actually yelling at
> Christy to get back to the table. Janet told me after a short while to
> just let her wander. Is this right? Part of me feels that she will al-
> ways think she can get away with not doing what she doesn't
> want to do. I'm finding it very hard to persuade a child to do les-
> sons, and this worries me.

The following day she finds the group easier to work with, despite the fact that some of them said the lesson was "boring." In comparing the two days, Kay notes that this group "seemed to want to read rather . . . than be elsewhere." She concludes, "I find for myself that if a child is trying and willing to put in the effort, I have a great deal of patience, but if they don't want to try, I don't know how to deal and I get very frustrated."

By the end of her fifth week, Kay has begun to realize that everything does not depend on the teacher, that there are many factors that influence what can and will occur. She seems to understand that developing skill in classroom management and teaching takes time. One cannot force children to learn, and learning will not always be fun. Children can contribute to their own learning, and observing them is beneficial. While it is important to plan, even the best of plans can go awry, but one can learn from a flop as well as from a success. Her embryonic theory of teaching and learning is now more apparent, and she shows evidence of applying ethical and moral criteria as she questions classroom events. However, it is important to note that although Kay has begun to collect material for reconstruction of prior preconceptions and implicit theories, she has not necessarily internalized the new way of thinking.

During her sixth week of teaching, what had gone "wonderfully yesterday" did not work. The children wanted to question when she wanted to cover material. "I really would have liked to get into a discussion of their questions, but there just wasn't time." She moves on, but the children balk:

> The whole class joined in and told me it was boring. I don't really remember what I said, something like, "Well, let's get through this and maybe the next thing we do you will enjoy" (or something to that effect). What do you do at this point? I really felt that it was not the entire class's feeling; they were just sort of joining in. If they really were bored with it, then yes, maybe I should have found a way to handle the lesson in a different way, but also the students unfortunately do have to do some things they don't want to, and if I don't do something when they say it's boring, they will begin to declare things boring before they give them a chance.

The expediency of coverage and control impinge on Kay's belief that learning should be fun. She continues to reflect on the experience, considering the possible consequences of giving in to their demand to quit because the lesson bored them, concluding that most of the children probably just went along with a few. The root of the problem, she assumes, is that "I could not keep the entire class quiet or listening or giving answers. I stopped in the middle, which was good, and explained that some people want to hear, so please let them. This worked for a little while, but the ruckus started again."

She summarizes what has become a lengthy journal entry with the hope that though the children may not have been happy at the moment, "this immediate feeling will pass, and they'll enjoy the big book" that they are preparing. This statement seems to reconcile her need for children to have fun with the more immediate need for social control.

Redefining Control

The tension between fun and control persists, and her reflection on it leads Kay to a new definition of control. Kay takes over the class when Janet is not feeling well. She writes, "I think on the whole I kept control of the classroom." She describes "favorite" moments that came during an activity in which she used a variety of manipulative and craft materials. "They all exclaimed about what fun they were having and how they wanted to do more stuff like this. . . . I liked the mixing of arts and crafts and intellectual skills." Later, in reflecting on the week, Kay writes:

> Through fun activities such as pumpkin carving, illustrating a poem, and other things, necessary concepts can be examined and understood. I am very much enjoying the challenge and creativity of integrated curricula, and I think they are a wonderful way to run a classroom.

Now Kay appears to be actually reconstructing her image of classroom control from one where the teacher is an authoritarian who keeps control to an image that ties control to curriculum planning and child development. This process seems to be strengthened when she observes children on a field trip and notices how much more relaxed she is in this context and how much she learns from seeing them in a different context.

Previously, in her autobiography, Kay noted how her own experience in an affluent suburban neighborhood contrasted to the experience of students in the after-school program in which she volunteered:

> They introduced me to the part of Ithaca I had never really seen. This was the part that was inhabited by the townies rather than the students of Cornell or Ithaca College. My mind became a great [deal] more opened this summer. I hope it can remain this way as I continue into the future.

As she nears the end of her first semester of student teaching, Kay begins to think more about the broader issues that were so compelling to her in Ithaca. Janet includes her in a conference with the parents of her child study subject, Violet. "This episode just pushed in my face again how much the family life affects a child and how important it is to ask questions about it. It certainly can lead to better understanding of the student and hopefully will help you deal with her better." After a parent night, she is reminded that "parents may teach their children differently than we do. Ideally a cooperation between teacher and parent should be set."

Kay's comments on these experiences are each examples of an opening for her to reflect on the ethical, political, and social implications of her work. While she seems to give little conscious attention to deliberative knowledge, she often analyzes events and assesses consequences with reference to moral and ethical criteria. For example, this is most evident as she begins to consider consequences of classroom decisions in terms of their immediate and long-term benefit to children. When children are grouped by skill level for reading, a practice she has begun to question even though it was fun for her as a child, she comments that sometimes it is needed "in order to keep interest and growth." When a lesson went "smoothly," but without everyone participating, Kay reflects:

> I did not try to get everybody to understand. I was happy when most did. Looking back I see that this is the easy way out. I know I was nervous and wanted it to work. So, I think for today this was okay, but for the future I will make more attempts to draw out the quiet students.

Here the moral criteria seems to be inclusiveness. She forgives herself for not involving everyone but will intentionally plan for participation. In another instance, what appears to be a rather technical focus is summarized by a comment in which she states that the activity will further show children that they know and can do a great deal.

Equity, fairness, and justice are clear themes that begin to appear in journal entries around the borders of her more compelling practical concerns. Early in the semester Kay has a strong reaction to an offhand jest that Janet makes about giving up on a child:

> At one point after class I asked Janet what to do about Christy, who says no to everything and is constantly causing trouble. She said in jest, "Oh, I've given up on her." But to me she's the one who least needs someone to give up on her. I know Janet is not totally giving up because I see her deal with her. I really don't want to be the type of teacher that gives up on kids, although I see how hard it is not to when you have 27 other students to think of. Idealistically, I'm saying I'll never give up, but I hope realistically I follow this.

The episode strikes at the heart of her sense of fair play, the theme of her early negative recollection. Kay comments on this episode in her reflection the following day, too, noting that Janet had spoken to a staff consultant about Christy and that they were working out ways of dealing with her. "I'm really glad about this. She needs the extra attention, and it's good to see Janet's not giving up on her as she quipped yesterday." Kay believes that Janet would not really give up on a child, but the incident evokes a strong reaction and a fear that it might happen. She also shows a growing awareness of the social realities of the classroom in her comment that *ideally* she will never give up. Perhaps she is beginning to see how teachers and schools can have a crushing effect on high ideals.

SIGNIFICANCE OF KAY'S PERSONAL KNOWLEDGE

Like most student teachers, Kay was concerned about herself, children, and activities and events of the classroom. Her writings show that she was most often concerned with actions, or who did what with or to whom, though she also dealt with feelings, values, and beliefs, particularly toward the end of her first semester. Her reflective style was primarily analytical. If Kay's degree of reflectivity were to be evaluated using the framework based on Van Manen's (1977) levels of reflectivity in curriculum, as they have been applied in studying the Wisconsin program (see Zeichner & Liston, 1987), we might conclude that she was largely technically oriented. Yet one can find instances in which she seems to make choices on the basis of strong value commitments and seems to be orienting herself for practical action. Despite the fact that she was eager to teach in urban schools and had the desire to help children, there are few instances that come close to Van Manen's highest level of reflective activity, which would have her questioning the worth of knowledge and the nature of social conditions that support one in raising such questions.

The focus of student teachers on themselves and their relationship to cooperating teachers, students, and the curriculum tends to preclude serious and penetrating, deliberative rationality, even though they may be motivated by social concerns. In concluding her review of literature on preservice and beginning teachers, Kagan (1992) notes that "the initial focus on self appears to be a necessary and crucial element in the first stage of teacher development. If this is true, then attempts by supervisors to shorten or abort a student teacher's period of inward focus may be counterproductive" (p. 155).

Confronting Personal Knowledge

Kay's first-semester experience confirms the significance of surfacing, critiquing, and beginning the process of reconstructing prior images of teaching. It is this work that, in a sense, clears the way for the development of an integrated view of theory, practice, and the moral dimensions of classroom/social control. Recognizing the power of personal knowledge may be the most significant work for a beginning student teacher, since all learning—including that about theory and its relation to curricular practice and classroom/social control—passes through the individual's mental and emotional filters.

We can see from Kay's experience that there are numerous opportunities for a student teacher to confront prior images and personal knowledge, to integrate theory and practice, and to come to terms with the broader implications of classroom control. But, to the extent that Kay is typical, we cannot expect that students—even strong students—will recognize and overcome negative factors in past experience and the powerful socializing impact of schools without particular kinds of support. Specific activities and experiences that required her to confront personal knowledge seemed to be helpful in moving Kay toward its critique and reconstruction. These are unlikely to be useful as recipes for teacher educators, however. More important than any particular technique is providing a context and climate for reflection through teacher education program activities and structures that recognize the social and cultural nature of personal knowledge. A context and climate of reflection provide student teachers with the opportunity to grow toward a greater capacity for deliberation.

At the same time, prospective teachers are naturally preoccupied with survival skills, such as classroom control. Hence it is crucial for teacher educators to maintain a dialectical tension between teacher needs (perceived and developmental) and a broader vision of teaching. Developmental theory—including work on teacher development and adult development—should serve not as a set of prescriptions for practice but as a useful lens from which to critique teacher preparation. Asking the penetrating question, probing for alternative ways of doing, and considering consequences are a few of the ways to do this.

Two instances from Kay's journal provide examples of maintaining the tension. The first is found in Kay's discussions of Christy, the child she feared Janet might give up on, and the second when she describes how the children declare that they are bored with her lesson.

In her discussion of Christy, we saw that Kay was disturbed about whether or not Janet would actually give up on a child, even though she recognized that Janet was jesting. Kay begins one of several reflections on Christy with a concern about classroom control. She does not know how to go about getting Christy to stay in her place and attend to a lesson. She has not yet begun to see how curricular choices have a profound effect on student behavior, nor does she yet recognize that Christy's restlessness may suggest that the planned activity is simply not reaching her. A technical response would be to provide her with an array of strategies for control—a direct response to her expressed need. In taking a broader view, her supervisor might engage her in a discussion about what could be prompting the behavior as well as strategies for dealing with Christy, thus addressing her concern but encouraging a more critical look at surface behavior.

Reorienting Personal Knowledge

When she describes her reaction to Janet's comment that she has "given up" on Christy, Kay already recognizes that Janet is unlikely really to give up. Her strong reaction is reflective of her own fears about how she will react to children who make her feel like giving up. Kay needs permission to express feelings about children, feelings that are negative as well as positive. Student teachers often need to be reassured that feelings are neutral; that is, they are not in themselves moral or immoral. Actions are not neutral.

Learning how to deal with the range of emotions that children evoke is one of the challenges of learning to teach. Yet teachers are offered little guidance in learning how to deal with the powerful feelings evoked in classroom life. Arthur Jersild's (1955) classic study, *When Teachers Face Themselves*, is a notable exception.

This instance in Kay's experience also suggests how a mental scaffolding could be built for more penetrating deliberation. Since Kay expresses a powerful emotional reaction to Janet's quip, she might be asked to consider why the incident evoked such a response. Kay's autobiography suggested a strong interest in social justice. Probing questions could lead her to a consideration of how children get labeled and who tends to be given up on by teachers and schools. The teacher educator's role is not to provide answers but to begin to develop the mental scaffold for such considerations in the future that will lead to positive moral choices. And, while it was not the case with Kay, her experience reminds us that where emotional reactions are out of proportion to the circumstance, the teacher educator needs to be sensitive to limitations and ready to make appropriate referrals.

As noted in Chapter 3, although teacher education literature has begun to explore the role of prior images in teaching, little has been done with the nature of images and how they relate to the emotional life of the classroom. Britzman (1986) looked at what appears to be the substance of images and their likely effect on teachers. Her work, too, is a reminder that memories contain content of experience and our perceptions and feelings that are related to the experience.

Teacher educators who are searching for ways to promote reflection should be aware that student teachers who do *not* have recall of early memories may not be ready for intense probing of experience without appropriate psychological support. Perhaps a broader vision for teacher educators will be one that has us working with colleagues in psychology and counseling education to explore deeper dimensions of reflection, including the place of emotions in learning to teach.

The second example of how Kay might have been helped to move toward deeper reflection can be found in the incident when the children declare that they are bored with the lesson she has planned and begin to balk. By this time in the semester, Kay is thinking about what she had planned and evaluates its appropriateness. She also wonders about whether or not children were really bored and whether they must always be excited about what they are learning, wrestling with what children want versus what they need. She may not be ready to analyze societal issues related to an entertainment-driven culture, but she might respond to a question such as "Where do you suppose they get that?" Again, the answer is less important than beginning to frame questions about classroom events and their broader implications.

CONCLUSION

In entering the classroom, student teachers are reentering a world of familiar social realities. They are already experts on teachers, students, and schools. But their expertise has been developed from the perspective of a student. A deliberative program needs to help student teachers see the classroom from multiple perspectives: of teacher, of children, of parents—both as remembered and as experienced in the present. When the conditions for genuine self-understanding, emancipatory learning, and deliberative rationality are present, the student teacher can begin to take on a new orientation. Questions such as how they are experiencing the classroom, how they have experienced classrooms in the past, how the cooperating teacher sees the classroom, and how it is seen by the children all provide material for the student teacher's reflection. Activities such as writing and discussing early recollections of school and their possible implications for teachers and students help promote encounter, which can lead to critique and later to accommodation and integration.

In part, teacher preparation is a process of reorientation to schools. Knowledge of how to observe and study children, classrooms, and schools is immediately applicable to the process of reorientation. Student teachers can begin, as Kay did, to see that issues of control, critical to teaching, may replicate repressive and authoritative structures or may be a means of creating structure and boundaries for students that allow them to increase control of their own behavior and to accept responsibility for actions. When this is the case, the moral attributes of respect, responsibility, and compassion are seen as essential tools for classroom community life. It is out of life together in the classroom that teachers are able to bring children into a kind of dialogue with the world around them and help them develop the tools for understanding and living in that world.

ಖ 5 ಜ

A Professional Community

> The internship year made my first years of teaching much
> smoother than they would have otherwise been. It let me
> develop my own ideas of how I wanted to do things while
> having a safety net below me. It taught me how to reach out
> to other teachers for help and to share ideas. I created a
> practice of working and planning with other teachers.
>
> —Kay, 1994

IN PREVIOUS CHAPTERS, we have looked at prospects for Kay's future as
a teacher and some of the barriers to learning to teach that she and other
academically able students face. She was described as being at risk of
dropping out of the profession. The focus thus far has been on preparation.
In this chapter, we make the transition to Kay's beginning years as a
teacher, looking at the conclusion of her student teaching, her internship
year, and her first year of teaching.

To understand her career trajectory, it is necessary to view Kay in
the unique context in which she gained her footing as a teacher. Kay
was one of the first student teachers to become an intern through TC's
professional development school partnership with District 3 of the New
York City Public Schools and the United Federation of Teachers, which
began in the late 1980s. It was in the PDS that she began her teaching
career as well.

THE PDS PARTNERSHIP

The PDS advocacy literature suggests that teacher education programs
that are connected to PDS partnerships are designed to develop and
promote reflective teachers. Collaboration, continuous learning, and inquiry into practice characterize reflective teaching (Pritchard & Ancess,
1999). Even though the Teachers College Preservice Program was de-

signed to promote these professional characteristics prior to the PDS partnership, Kay's experience was not typical of other TC graduates, by virtue of her involvement in the PDS. For one thing, she spent more hours in the school than other student teachers. And she was part of the mix as the PDS partnership evolved.

At the outset, the Elementary School Partnership Planning Team (including the school principal, three teachers, and TC program director) envisioned a 3-year process for preservice teachers. It would include the program coursework, two semesters of student teaching, and a year of internship. The internship was to be guided by two mentor teachers who had already begun collaborative teaching and learning activities during the start-up year. The intern would become part of the team, working within and across homeroom groups with mentor teachers. As the internship concluded, interns would be expected to assume full teaching responsibility for one of the homeroom groups for at least 6 weeks. During this period, mentor teachers would share responsibility for the remaining homeroom group, freeing each other for at least 3 weeks of other professional activities. Upon completion of the internship, interns were to be placed as beginning teachers in schools within District 3 and receive support from their internship mentors during their initial year (see Snyder, 1994, for a more detailed account of the partnership).

The Partners

Even before the PDS partnership, TC preservice faculty had spent time in schools working with student teachers and cooperating teachers. However, the program image suffered from TC's poor reputation with New York City public schools, which was fueled by both myth and reality. One persistent myth was that TC could and ought to rescue city schools from their multiple, complex problems. Another was that TC could and would use its high status within the world education community to impose its will on the schools. The conflicting wishes, expectations, fears, and resentment of TC as "savior" led to a climate of suspicion and hostility. Neither myth was without some basis in reality. For example, one of the administrators in the PDS had completed her preservice preparation at TC more than a decade before without doing any field work. Teaching skills were developed through learning and peer-teaching various models of teaching. During the several years in which she was associated with the project, this administrator clung to the belief that universities are only concerned with theoretical matters, though she allowed that the partnership was an exception. Several teachers were familiar with the school improvement model of intervention from colleges and universities

and had chaffed under various college-dominated curriculum-implemen-
tation efforts. The school ethos included the wide perception that universities were theoretical and schools dealt with concrete, practical realities.
As Naomi Hill, the principal who was part of the initial planning group,
expressed it:

> I found my faculty took it very seriously. We discussed it a lot. A
> lot of presentations. You know, "Why should we do it?" Teachers
> really feel more professional when they're buddying with the uni-
> versity. I think it's a love/hate relationship. They think the univer-
> sity is in la-la land and unrealistic. On the other hand, there's a
> tremendous awe and respect.

The initial elementary partner school (PDS hereafter) was located on
Manhattan's Upper West Side a block from the American Museum of
Natural History. The neighborhood has become one of the more desirable
locations in the city, as evidenced by upscale brownstones and trendy
boutiques, restaurants, and coffee shops. In 1990, however, there were
also crowded, deteriorating tenement houses and abandoned, junk-filled
lots within the same community. The contrast between rich and poor is
still visible despite the press of gentrification, though the contrast was
much more pronounced in the early 1990s. The school was built in 1954
and reflects the typical egg-crate design of its time.

When Kay began her internship, there were approximately 1,100
students in kindergarten through grade 5 and a faculty of 58 teachers.
The principal had begun with a failing city school, building it into a vital
professional community through rigorous efforts to recruit children and
their families, careful selection and development of teachers, and a progressive vision that insisted on diversity, active learning, integrated curriculum, academic excellence, and school as community. Even though the
faculty was not entirely hand-picked, it was, by and large, an empowered
group. Most had been trained in a progressive tradition that emphasized
building curriculum from the needs and interests of the child and valued
practical, hands-on approaches to learning (Snyder, 1994). In keeping with
Hill's commitment to shared decision making, becoming part of the PDS
was discussed with teachers:

> They decided that those who wanted to be involved would be in-
> volved. Those who didn't, wouldn't have to be but would not stop
> the others. In other words, you didn't have to have the whole fac-
> ulty to do it or not do it. And that was significant. The original
> group was very enthusiastic. As I say, they really kind of reorga-

nized themselves into pairs and did all this changing of curriculum.

It should be noted, however, that the elementary school partner was not an alternative or charter school. Hill pointed out, "We abide by the rules that govern every city school." This meant that she had to accept transfer teachers from within the system and live with bureaucratic restrictions from which many highly successful alternative schools were exempt. This was an important, conscious decision on Hill's part:

> Until we can show that change is possible within the boundaries every school has to live with, we will never change the system. We'll only provide a rich experience for the precious few lucky enough to be part of an alternative arrangement. If the rules don't work, we don't solve the problem by exempting a few people from them. We have to work together to change the rules. I feel very strongly about this.

Hill's commitment to making the system work involved a comprehensive staff development program. She personally visited, urged, and encouraged every teacher to become more child centered and provided staff development and resource personnel to help them improve their craft. In extreme cases, where a teacher seemed too weak to be in the classroom and was not amenable to staff development, she worked out alternative responsibilities outside the classroom that provided additional services to the school and all teachers. In the words of one teacher, Hill was "constantly in your face."

Kay's PDS Experience

Kay was accepted as a student teacher in the PDS along with about 18 peers. Interns were to be selected from student teachers during the second semester of student teaching. They were to demonstrate their commitment to teaching in urban schools, show a high degree of competence in student teaching, and work effectively as members of their curriculum teams within the school and in the program core. There was a great a deal of discussion about whether the internship should serve people who were already successful or who were less successful. In the end, it was determined that either might be the case, but interns should be people who demonstrated eagerness to learn and would profit from the experience. Kay was one of two interns selected at the end of the spring term of student teaching. In her case, it was agreed that she showed a great deal of competence as well as the capacity to continue to learn.

The model was seen as luxurious by potential funders and was pared down to a much leaner version in its third year. Kay was one of four graduates who actually completed the year-long student teaching and internship at the elementary school level. No one denied the benefits of the model. But no one seemed to want to pay for it. Kay was employed at the school following her internship, and the assistant principal described her as "light years ahead of other beginning teachers," pointing out that "she has a sophistication that teachers don't usually acquire until well into their third or fourth year."

The literature on PDS partnerships talks about the benefits of PDS relationships and the enriched environment they provide for neophyte teachers (Pritchard & Ancess, 1999). While rich and nurturing, the school environment Kay entered was not without problems. As a student teacher and intern, Kay was directly in the "line of fire" as the PDS relationship was being negotiated. Relationships among the partners were often difficult and contentious. In fact, the PDS was characterized as much by conflict as by cooperation during its formative years (see Snyder, 1992). Many of the areas of conflict went directly to the heart of what it means to prepare and support teachers. Kay was on hand for schoolwide PDS meetings as well as being witness to countless faculty room and hallway conversations about the PDS. Many of these conversations cast her college program in an unfavorable light, although interns and student teachers were not always conscious of the contentious nature of the relationship.

WHO OWNS WHAT KNOWLEDGE?

The relationship between theory and practice—who owned what knowledge?—was one of the most vexing and persistent issues the school faced. Ideally, reform of schools, teaching, and teacher education should be the result of a "collaborative synergy" that occurs when university and school people collaborate (Snyder, 1994, p. 118). True collaboration shows respect for knowledge of the other. But true collaboration is an ideal won by working through the conflict that inevitably emerges. The act of engaging in collaboration often brings the darker tendencies of the individual members of a group to the surface. Subtle and not-so-subtle battles over power and control occur and can preoccupy and divert a group from its avowed purpose. Real differences in mission, purposes, and motives can become sources of irritation.

The issue of ownership of knowledge has been such a common one that PDS partnerships have made it a specific goal "to develop coherence between the theory of the university and the practice of the school-based studies" (Pritchard & Ancess, 1999, p. 6). In summarizing literature on PDS partnerships, Pritchard and Ancess comment that in the best of situations,

> the teacher candidate is placed with a cohort of interns into the care and guidance of a team of experienced professionals, both school-based and university-based. Seminars, discussion groups, demonstration lessons, team teaching, and joint planning are common features of PDS internships. Thus, from the onset of their education as teachers, PDSs offer pre-service candidates the opportunity to join multiple professional communities, thereby providing an alternative expectation that contrasts with the conventional model of teacher isolation and privatized practice. (p. 7)

The studies advocating placement of students in PDSs versus traditional preservice teacher education tend to confirm the perspective Pritchard and Ancess describe. However, arriving at a place where theory and practice are seamless requires more than establishing a PDS. Many players in a partnership have to accommodate a view in which theory and practice are interrelated, not the "property" of either university or school.

The theory–practice challenge presented itself in various ways that permeated the intellectual and social climate surrounding Kay. In many instances, the terms *theory* and *practice* seemed to be based on vague role expectations rather than on any substantive difference between theorizing and the practice of teaching. Two examples illustrate the vague notions about who should theorize and who should practice: the orientation for intern candidates and creation of the role of clinical faculty. Both have direct bearing on Kay's experience.

Orienting Intern Candidates

Teachers at the school wanted to kick off the PDS program by having an on-site orientation to the school for all student teachers, including Kay, who would be candidates for the internship. The planning team agreed that this could be an effective way to begin, charging a committee of two senior teachers, Susan and Ellie, with developing a "hands-on" orientation workshop. The workshop was to include site-specific knowledge about the school and general knowledge about being a student teacher. Susan and Ellie spoke with the planning committee about their interest in supplementing the college's more "theoretical" approach with "real school" activities. Both were direct and open in sharing their conviction that without the orientation, student teachers and interns would be hopelessly impractical in their approach to teaching and learning.

The workshop, as it turned out, emphasized many topics covered in core in ways remarkably similar to methods used in core. Although student teachers had been placed at the school for more than a decade prior to the PDS partnership, the workshop reflected little awareness of what we actually do in the preservice program. Rather than focusing on the school, Susan and Ellie planned a variety of activities to get student teachers to think about their role as teachers—activities that overlapped with core. The similarity between the workshop and core suggested "some kind of misconception that we sit around talking about theory" at the college, as I noted at the time.

The attitudes of school faculty permeated the school and spilled over into the core in subtle ways. In some cases spillover took the form of passive resistance. For example, there were cooperating teachers who offered student teachers little support in completing core assignments that were dependent on being in the field, such as the child study. Whether or not they commented on core assignments in a negative way, their attitudes were difficult to miss. Others, like Susan, who became Kay's cooperating teacher during her second semester of student teaching, were not in agreement with many of the core assignments but maintained a professional stance by keeping any misgivings to themselves. Others were open and positive about working with the program and ready to support student teachers in any way they could, particularly those teachers who became members of the clinical faculty at TC.

Involving Clinical Faculty

The planning committee had agreed early in the project that certain PDS teachers, designated as clinical faculty, should be involved in the program core rather than being invited to give guest lectures or teach stand-alone methods courses. By visibly working together as a team, we could do a great deal to erase some of the status boundaries that seem to exist between college and elementary school teachers and strengthen the collaboration. Furthermore, while only a few of our students would have access to the PDS as a learning site, the benefits of the partnership could be shared with all students through interaction with clinical faculty. More significantly, to make a difference in how teachers are educated, the partnership needed to have input into the heart of the program, the year-long core, described in Chapter 1. The principal agreed to release a teacher to attend planning meetings and teach core. To maximize planning time with clinical faculty, preservice planning meetings were held on site at the school. The planning meetings addressed program issues as well as planning and assessment of core. With the exception of these structural agreements, the role of clinical faculty was not defined but left open to co-construction by preservice and clinical faculty with feedback from preservice students.

Co-construction began when Merry and Trish, two of the teachers who had been part of the PDS effort from its initial organizational meeting, were interested in serving as clinical faculty. But they wanted to know whether they could split the position. As we talked it through, this seemed like a sensible idea. There were numerous advantages. After the start-up year, an experienced clinical faculty member could team with a new member. It would also allow maximum participation of school faculty over time and provide program continuity. And it made the job seem less daunting to both Merry and Trish. They were appointed as adjunct instructors by the college and halved the usual salary for an adjunct.

Expanding Conceptions of Theory

The relationship of theory to practice surfaced almost immediately. As we talked about what the role of clinical faculty might be, we all agreed that, like all new instructors in the program, clinical faculty would observe and study the program initially, offering suggestions in planning meetings and feeling free to take on teaching tasks as they felt comfortable doing so. They could jump in and add ideas or insights during core discussions at any time. In this sense, their role in core was parallel to that of new preservice instructors.

Merry and Trish both spoke of their role as being one of bringing practical ideas into the core. Trish commented, "You have to understand that I know next to nothing about the theoretical. I am very practical. I'm a little nervous about that part of it."

In later planning meetings, Trish described herself more than once as someone who did not "have the theories down." At the same time, her talk and classroom practice were both reflective of strong commitments to constructivist theory. Merry, on the other hand, seemed comfortable with direct talk about theory, did not seem to draw boundaries between theory and practice, and described herself as constructivist.

In the debriefing session following our first meeting of the core, Trish expressed surprise at how "practical" the session seemed to be. "Somehow I didn't expect that of a university."

The idea that universities owned theory and schools practice persisted. Other teachers were less polite than Trish was. Norma, one of the cooperating teachers, made comments at a PDS meeting that expressed a common view. After describing the core syllabus as too hard to follow and too prescriptive, Norma said, "Nothing TC does has anything to do with the reality of what goes on in classrooms." From her perspective, the entire student-teaching and intern experience should be worked out between the cooperating teacher and supervisor without "interference" from the university. For most PDS teachers, partnership did not mean shared control, but reversing the power roles. Their formal and informal discussions about issues related to the PDS often included a great deal of "TC bashing."

As a student teacher and, later, as an intern, Kay describes herself as "oblivious" to the negative attitude teachers held toward the college. "I complained about the workload along with everybody else," but Janet, her cooperating teacher for the first semester of student teaching, "was a graduate of the program and very sympathetic. She supported all my assignments." During the second semester, Susan was "not so [much] sympathetic as tolerant" of core assignments.

Furthermore, feeding the theory–practice schism was the principal's inadvertent use of the "college as savior" myth as a rallying point for teachers. By and large, teachers both expected TC to use its influence to provide top-down solutions to urban school problems and, at the same time, resented interference by the college in their affairs. Most teachers agreed that the college was uninterested in the real world of practice and could not be expected to do the right thing without constant surveillance. In this way, teachers were enlisted to focus on internal improvements. As Hill urged in one meeting, "We can't sit around waiting for TC to do this. We have to do it for ourselves." The overall effect was what Snyder (1994) described as the reverse of a school-improvement approach to change; that is, the school saw itself as the agent to change the university.

Conflicting Expectations

Traditional models of educational change have focused on school improvement. The school improvement program (SIP) model feeds the "college as savior" myth because it focuses on correcting situations or practices that are leading to poor school performance, whether these be skills of teachers, curriculum, or leadership factors. It makes the assumption that deficits in the school can be corrected from the top down, with assistance by outside experts (usually from the university). Initially, one teacher wondered, "Will we have to follow TC's philosophy? Is a TC supervisor going to tell me that I should do thus and so?" (quoted in Snyder, 1994, p. 119).

In describing the PDS partnership in which Kay was involved, Snyder (1994) points to what he named the "Flip-SIP," or the inverse of the school improvement program model, "the notion that the school people own all the knowledge that counts and that the college people are the ones in need of saving" (p. 120). School people saw the college as deficient and their role as one of changing the college. While both partners had overlapping interests—providing education for children—there were "differing fundamental interests" and points of accountability (p. 121). The preservice faculty looked to the school to provide students of teaching a model of lifelong learning in which teachers continued to learn from their craft. They hoped teachers would reflect an experimental attitude toward teaching and learning and induct student teachers into the knowledge and skills of teaching. Teachers were focused primarily on their students and expected student teachers to have practical knowledge of teaching and learning that would benefit students and provide them with "an extra pair of hands" in the classroom. While teachers were eager to share knowledge and skills, most expected student teachers to come with a repertoire of skills. Teachers' expectations seemed more in keeping with an undergraduate model that equips preservice students with methods courses and practicum experiences *prior* to student teaching.

As a student teacher, Kay was being asked to focus on two different sets of goals that reflected the differences in the fundamental interests of the PDS partners. The college wanted her to become a deliberative practitioner, and the school wanted her to be a skilled practitioner. Simply put, the college wanted student teachers to ask "why," and the school wanted student teachers to know "how."

OWNING HER OWN KNOWLEDGE

Midway through her second semester of student teaching in a fourth-grade class, Kay experiences firsthand the conflict that cooperating teachers felt in their role involving commitment to children and their role as teacher of teachers. She wonders why she is allowed to observe only one parent–teacher conference when she was fully involved with all of the conferences during her first semester. Recognizing that parents might feel uncomfortable or defensive when there are sensitive issues, she conjectures that if Susan had asked the parents, some might have allowed her to participate. Kay does not recall whether or not she discussed this issue with Susan at the time, nor does she refer to it in her student-teaching journal. It would have been in keeping with Susan's style to talk about it, however. Susan was highly professional, supportive of student teachers, and gave them a great deal of attention. But she did believe that her first responsibility was to the children. Snyder (1994) noticed the underlying tension in experiences such as Kay's, commenting:

Teachers defined themselves as good teachers because they gave their all to children which meant being with children constantly. Two of the major rewards they received were the pleasure of being with children, and the ability, when in their classrooms, to be the sole adult responsible for constructing classroom reality. A PDS demanded a new role for teachers—one for which most were neither emotionally nor professionally prepared. (pp. 114–115)

Despite internal tensions within the PDS, the partners attempted to form an authentic collaboration. The environment at the PDS provided an exceptionally rich and supportive context for Kay's development as a teacher. And, while there were experiences in both Susan's and Janet's classrooms that were frustrating to her as a student teacher, Kay remembers more that were positive and nurturing.

Developing an Experimental Mindset

Although Kay noted that she was largely oblivious to the political strain within the PDS partnership, there were times when she seemed to be buying into the negative view of TC. Kay remembers complaining to peers and her supervisor about the tensions between fulfilling requirements for core and staying on top of things in the classroom. But it is clear from examination of her second semester of student teaching and internship experience that the dispositions that were fostered throughout her program were beginning to "take."

As we saw earlier, by the end of her first semester of student teaching, she had begun to surface and critique her own personal knowledge. The rigorous child study project completed during first semester had become more than "just another assignment" to Kay. She realized that it was equipping her to be a student of teaching.

In her second semester, Kay begins to refine an experimental mindset about teaching that becomes characteristic of her career. She poses problems for herself and forms hypotheses about the effects of her behavior and teaching strategies. Her skill in observation is apparent in a second child study for her independent master's project.

During the first week of the second semester, Kay volunteers to take on a 3-week science curriculum on sound because she is "not one who loves science" and believes that she can learn from it. She also works with a child who makes repeated mistakes in solving arithmetic problems and questions the child's apparent inability to learn from mistakes. She notices that every time he begins a new arithmetic problem, he seems to approach it as something new, apparently failing to see the relationship among problems. She makes a note to follow up on the intervention she has used to "see if he got it and will retain it." Kay speculates about a child who is ahead of the others in her reading group but does not contribute. "He comprehends fine, so I would like to work on getting past just the plot with him." She considers several strategies to explore whether he is getting more out of the text than she suspects and determines to keep a watchful eye on him.

In the first semester, Kay began to question how to create and sustain a curriculum based on student interests, puzzling through how to deal with content that the children may find boring but that they need to know. The question emerges again when she tries to elicit what the children would like to learn in the science unit on sound and they do not respond. "This makes me think about how a purely student-initiated curriculum might be hard to keep going at times. The teacher would have to initiate some activities and experiences that can point out different aspects of the topics." As she continues to think about this issue, her reading group pleasantly surprises Kay. She explains to the children that they are behind where they should be and asks what could be done about it. She agrees to let them try their suggestions and notes, "When I presented it to them as a problem that wasn't their fault and something that posed a challenge, they all rallied together to solve it. I'm very interested to see if they stick to it."

Kay's strategy becomes a pattern—describing a situation, posing it as a problem that can be solved, and planning what to do differently. At the close of the semester, Kay wrote in her self-evaluation, "I try to consider all problems that might emerge. . . . I apply what occurs in one lesson to my next lesson and include evaluation techniques in my lessons." This attitude is a clearly identifiable, conscious part of Kay's repertoire as a mature teacher as well.

As the semester progresses we see Kay taking on an experimental mindset. She merges theoretical and practical aspects of teaching and projects herself into the role of teacher as learner. At the same time, Kay wrestles with "old voices" from her past experiences as a student and continues to reconstruct these experiences.

Dealing with Hearing Old Voices

More than halfway through her second semester of student teaching, Kay experiences what seems to be a disaster. She is teaching the whole class during the last part of the day and students become noisy, restless, and disruptive. After reprimanding them, she decides to be silent. All of the children become quiet except Emma, who talks "in a funny way." Kay gives her a forceful look, but when Emma says something funny, Kay laughs in spite of herself. The whole class explodes with laughter. When she finally gets them calmed down, Emma disrupts again. This time the class "all started laughing and being 10 times as noisy as they were before." Kay has no patience left. She yells at Emma. Then, to regain control of the class, she threatens that the cooperating teacher will test them on the material they are supposed to be covering. She immediately feels that she has done the wrong thing. She has been inconsistent by "laughing one minute and yelling the next." She adds, reflecting on the consequences of threatening them, "I hate doing something like this because they shouldn't think of learning to be only because they'll have to know it for a test."

Kay is very clear about her feelings and is able to pinpoint when the breakdown in behavior occurs as a result of her own actions. She decides that what she should have done was to comment that Emma's remark was really funny but that the timing was not appropriate and to ask her not to disrupt again. Kay has examined the problem and projected a better solution than the one that spontaneously emerged. But her reflection goes further. "I did so many things I know I don't want to do as a teacher purely because I was upset because I knew I had lost control and was upset with myself."

This is a significant moment for Kay. She is able to assess her mistakes and determine a course of future action. But more significant is how Kay's spontaneous response is consistent with her own experiences as a student in classrooms that were characterized by control. While she has not consciously made the connection between her spontaneous behavior and past classroom experiences, she is aware of the tension between what she wants to do and what she seems to do in the heat of the moment. This is an important part of the reconstruction process.

Constructing Self as the Teacher

Susan's tension with the role of cooperating teacher is apparent when a set of scales is broken during Kay's science lesson. Three children were involved and, predictably, blamed each other. Kay decides to put the scales aside and continue "so [as] not to hold up class," but Susan, who had stepped out of the room, "walked back in and started yelling about the scale." Kay explains that she will talk to those involved after students begin to work independently. Later, when she calls them over and begins to talk:

> Emily was crying, and the others were blaming her. After about 5 minutes, I had Emily calmed down and the three of them admitting that they were playing with the scale when they shouldn't

have been and therefore were all to blame. At this point Susan came over and demanded they go in the hall and had her own talk with them.

I really feel that since I was doing the lesson that I should have been the one to discuss the matter with the students and then consult Susan on what she wanted them to do. I thought I was handling the situation nicely by not spotlighting them in front of the whole class and by discussing it.

In her weekly reflection, Kay is still apparently smarting from the experience. She begins by thinking about how "having more than one adult in the class can cause conflicting messages, but this led me to think about how next year there won't be another adult at all." The experience becomes a springboard for thinking about herself as a teacher. She returns to her concern about how to handle child-centered curriculum. Being alone in the classroom will "make it hard to implement the methods I tend to rely on, such as small groups and hands-on."

This is a watershed moment for Kay. From this point she seems to be separating herself from Susan and thinking about what she will want in a school environment. She continues to worry about being the only adult in the classroom. "Hopefully I will be able to develop relationships with a group of teachers in whatever school I'm in that will share materials and also ideas. I'm sure this will be easier or more difficult depending on the school and its social context." She talks about her résumé and the job search in weekly reflections thereafter. And there is a noticeable difference in how she articulates her experience in writing and in talking about teaching. Things are coming together.

The issues of social justice that motivated her to think about teaching as a career choice begin to resurface as the end of second semester approaches. She is working on a curriculum with a group of students in core and trying out some of the lessons with her reading group. They are looking at the life of Helen Keller, and Kay works on "getting them to become aware that physically disabled people have many problems that we take totally for granted." She delights in a student-initiated discussion of how society does not even think about the obstacles that are in the way of physically disabled people. She is deeply disappointed, however, when students do not apply the concept of accepting differences by making an attempt to befriend Chuck, a new student. Not only do they fail to relate their insights about how people fail to care for others to Chuck, they show little sympathy for him when he is acting out. The situation becomes a crisis for her when Chuck starts making noises during her social studies lesson. Children complain, and twice she asks him to stop.

When he repeats the behavior, she asks him to leave the group. "Many of the students started applauding as Chuck left. It was horrible. Chuck started crying. . . . I could not believe they were soooo cruel."

The next day, Susan talks with the class about not teasing and name-calling. Kay notices that while there is no overt negative behavior from other children, none offer Chuck friendship. Again, she is troubled by what happens in her social studies lesson. "We were talking about rules and Chuck kept turning the discussion toward a hypothetical new student who doesn't know the rules or isn't close to anybody and what they should do. He kept coming back to it even after the students gave him answers such as ask other students or teachers." Two days later, as she asks the children to talk about which parts of the Bill of Rights are most important to them. "Chuck decided the most important one was the ability to sue those that say lies about him." Again, Chuck talks in terms of a hypothetical child, this time saying how a student can have a rumor spread about him and everybody believes it.

Unfortunately, Kay does not see the situation to a happy resolution. Chuck's parents oppose special supports for him, and classroom solutions do not seem powerful enough to make a difference. She does notice, however, how attentively Susan continues to work with parents and follow up with resource personnel and vows to show equal diligence when she has her own classroom. She sees that, like Janet during her first semester, Susan is unwilling to give up on a child.

Her last journal entry speaks of her new confidence and eagerness to have her own classroom. She reflects on the many ideas she has been exposed to:

> I want to accomplish things and do things I never thought of be-
> fore I student-taught. There are so many ideas I want to try in my
> own classroom that I can't imagine how I'll get everything done. I
> have to convince myself that I can't do everything my first year. It
> will have to be built up slowly. But I'm so anxious to try out *Every-*
> *thing*!! Let's just hope I have a job to try them at come September.

Kay's fears were put to rest when she was offered one of two coveted internships in the PDS for the year following her student teaching.

THE INTERNSHIP

For her internship Kay remained with the team where she had student-taught spring semester, with Susan and Ellie serving as her mentor teachers. Interns were ultimately selected by the school principal, based on recommendations by TC faculty and PDS teachers. In order to provide continuity of experience for the interns, PDS partners agreed that mentor teachers would be those cooperating teachers who had worked with interns during the second semester of student teaching. Naomi Hill was pleased to have both Susan and Ellie guiding Kay. "I had enormous respect for them, their judgment, their professionalism."

The tension Kay experienced in wanting to do more than Susan was ready for her to do as a student teacher continued into the internship year and is captured in the advice she offers for new interns who will follow her: "Know you are not going to be the honcho." Since Kay was one of only two groups of student teachers who were able to complete a year of internship following student teaching, it is not surprising that the experience was not fully developed. In a personal communication in January 2001, Jon Snyder described it as "an extended student-teaching experience for her. . . . It was a slow entry approach. She was not a co-teacher with a reduced teaching load as I would argue is appropriate for most beginning teachers."

Remarkably Different Mentors

Jon, who had been an instructor in the program and was documenting the PDS, had much more direct contact with Kay than anyone else from the college during the internship year. (In fact, many of the comments about the internship are drawn from the extensive notes he took that year.) As the other faculty partner, I was also at the school one or two days a week. Both Susan and Ellie, who were the mentor teachers in her internship team, were "feeling their way." Susan was more experienced and nurturing, while Ellie was still concerned about her role and constantly had to deal with her "impulse to rescue." While both teachers could be described as reflective about their practice, each played a different role in mentoring Kay. Susan helped Kay to develop her practice and provided her with ways of analyzing students and their work. Kay relied on Susan for emotional support. Despite any uncertainties she may have had about the role, Ellie was more articulate and intellectual about her teaching practice. "Though their styles differed, Kay had some pretty remarkable models," Jon explained.

The uncertainty that Ellie was experiencing did not escape Kay. "Ellie was definitely learning a supervisory style. She was constantly trying things," as Jon recalls. Kay talks about the difficulty she experienced in working with two teachers, each with different styles. The two had teamed during her student-teaching year and she had exposure to Ellie's teaching.

But she rarely spent time with Ellie, nor did she receive supervision from Ellie. The internship year was structured such that Kay and Ellie each had a homeroom class. Susan was the swing teacher between both classes but basically set up the classroom and management structures for Kay's homeroom. Ellie handled the math and science for both homerooms, and Susan handled the social studies and language arts. Kay recalls that Ellie was always coming in when she was teaching and interrupting or taking over to demonstrate the "correct" approach and/or finish the lesson. This was hard for Kay to adjust to. "I just wasn't prepared for the different styles of two people who were supposed to be collaborating."

Kay felt that Ellie wanted to impose her style on the classroom, even though it was set up following Susan's guidance and preferences. Kay had rationalized the adjustment to Susan during her second semester of student teaching on the grounds that there was such an age difference between the first grade, where she had been first semester, and Susan's fourth grade. Now she was learning that style, more than the age difference of the children, accounted for the differences, since both Susan and Ellie taught fourth grade and both could be described as constructivist in their approach.

While Jon appreciated Ellie's intellectual grasp of teaching practice, Kay saw Ellie as a great thinker who was always starting out with large plans that were in her head but were not communicated to Kay. During her second semester, Kay had chaffed when Susan took over disciplining children who got into an argument over a broken set of scales. Her reaction was even stronger to Ellie's interventions, particularly when she took over a lesson.

Kay still remembers the somewhat raw feelings she had when Ellie injected herself into a lesson. But now she is able to laugh as she tells me, "Ellie may not have done it more than a couple of times, but it seemed like more! It just left me feeling frustrated and embarrassed, particularly if I was trying something I hadn't ever done before." Ellie usually had an idea in her mind of how she wanted things done, whereas Susan was more flexible. Furthermore, Ellie didn't always follow through with her big schemes and, as a new teacher, "I needed a beginning, middle, and end to things." Being interrupted in front of the children "made me feel as if wasn't really a teacher." As Jon recalls:

> Kay liked working with Susan because she felt like a teacher with Susan and not like a teacher with Ellie. Susan, it should be noted, did provide considerable teaching practices content to Kay (including pretty in-depth analysis of students and student work), so it

wasn't that she was just the proverbial shoulder to cry on. She just had a softer approach than Ellie and was experienced enough in the role to know when not to intervene.

Ellie gained footing as a teacher of teachers, and Kay became savvy at interpreting her preferences. "There was a point where she quit taking over. By the end of the year I felt more like a teacher."

Hill, respecting Susan and Ellie for what each brought to the situation, remembers:

> Susan was the most centered, probably the best practitioner I had ever worked with, always knew how to work with every kid. She was a natural. And Ellie was so thoughtful and had all these built-in systems but somehow maybe had more issues. . . . Ellie was re-thinking every minute—an introspective teacher. But very different than Susan. Susan was very centered, very steady. Her class was always working. There were never issues there. But Ellie tried to invent herself every day.

A Good Enough Model

As a collaborative model, the internship was only partially successful. Susan and Ellie worked together to guide Kay. But there was little role for TC. Jon recalls, "Interestingly, in the entire year she *never* said anything about a potential role for a college person in the internship. There was no college role." As she ended her internship, Kay explained to Jon, "Fran was there if needed, but she wasn't needed. I can't really see any need for a college role in the internship unless the teacher match wasn't working. Maybe you need somebody there to report to, to intervene if needed, but that doesn't have to be a college person."

This reflects the experience as I recall it, too. As a college-based member of the partnership, I began spending about two days a week at the school when the internships started. Yet I saw Kay minimally. I spent far more time with the second intern, negotiating conflict the team was experiencing in other classrooms in the building. Since my colleague, Jon, had established rapport with Kay's team, I took a hands-off approach. As Kay put it, I was there if she needed me. My contact with all the members of Kay's team was through brief, informal stops in the home-room, at meetings, or in the hall.

In reflecting on the experience, Kay is aware that the internship was being invented when she experienced it and the PDS never had the opportunity to refine the model. Lack of funding forced a new pattern that identifies interns from the beginning and places them in the classroom for a modified and extended student-teaching experience. Kay believes the internship gave her additional experience, but working between the two teachers with different styles was complicating. Kay thinks now that intensive support during the beginning year of teaching would be more beneficial. Perhaps, had the internship developed along the lines that were initially imagined, she would have been a co-teacher and experienced many of the challenges of first-year teachers in an enriched environment. While the idea was conceptually sound, the internship possibilities created by enriched staffing were not used as productively as they might have been. While both mentor teachers respected Kay, they did not view her as a full-fledged teacher. The result, as Jon recalls, was that "there was less of a push to creative uses of the possibilities . . . which the data made very evident."

At the same time, Kay realized many benefits from the experience, not the least of which was a job at the school when the internship ended. Three years after the fact, Kay describes the experience as unique, one that "very few first-year teachers are able to have. It enabled me to slowly take more and more responsibility for instruction, curriculum development, record keeping, and social development of the classroom."

Whatever its limitations, Kay emerged from the internship as a highly respected beginning teacher. Her location within the PDS allowed a more seamless transition into her beginning year. Susan, who retired at the end of the internship year, was designated as her mentor during the beginning year, in keeping with the model. Kay could look forward to her support. And she had also met other members of the fourth-grade team. One of them, Jason, was just finishing his first year. Before the internship came to an official close, Kay and Jason had agreed to collaborate on curriculum in the coming year.

"GROWING UP" PDS

Literature on the impact of PDSs on teacher learning suggests that teachers do indeed benefit from being part of a PDS. Abdal-Haqq (1998, cited in Pritchard & Ancess, 1999) identifies the several benefits reported by teachers. These include (1) willingness to take instructional risks and experiment, (2) intellectual stimulation from new ideas and opportunities to engage in activities such as school-based research and collegial interactions, (3) engaging in nontraditional roles, (4) less sense of isolation, (5) less sense of powerlessness, (6) improvement in classroom practice, and (7) greater sense of professionalism.

While there is still a great deal to learn about the functioning of PDSs, it is notable that they exemplify the new roles for teachers. They share the characteristics used to describe highly functional schools in literature on school reform. That is, they see themselves as a professional community, share norms and values, focus on student learning, emphasize reflective dialogue, encourage collaborative and cooperative practices in classrooms and among faculty, and claim a sense of control over working conditions (Pritchard & Ancess, 1999).

Even with the benefit of a full-year internship, Kay was not spared from the challenges of a first-year teacher. Management, organization, and discipline were problems. "Keeping up with attendance and all the paper work was unbelievably time consuming." Kay remembers once she was so frustrated with the class that she walked out and slammed the classroom door. To her embarrassment, Susan, on her way to see how Kay was doing, saw it happen. Kay doesn't recall what was said, but having Susan there was a benefit. She felt reassured rather than judged.

During the first year she had a good grasp of expectations and could be self-critical, but "I just couldn't juggle all the pieces." At that point, "I knew what I should be doing and what I was doing wrong."

Despite her perception of having struggled, those around her saw her strengths. As noted earlier, the assistant principal described her as "light years ahead of most beginners." Susan had set up the internship classroom, and her authority and structure were there from the beginning. Once in her own room, authority and structure had to be established by Kay alone, however. Initially, Kay modeled her classroom after Susan's. "As time passed I began to say, 'We're going to rearrange the room because it isn't working for us,' you know, that kind of thing. So that by the end of the year it really was more my own classroom."

There were times when Kay wished her program had provided her with more specific techniques about how to set up the classroom and establish routines and more teaching strategies and had deemphasized the experimental mindset. But as time passed, she began to realize that she was equipped to learn from her teaching and create appropriate classroom routines and strategies. And she had some skills that other beginning teachers did not have.

Perhaps the thing that set her apart from most beginning teachers was her grasp of the curriculum. From the beginning, Kay collaborated with other teachers. She and Jason began immediately to work together to plan their fourth-grade curriculum. In fact, Kay does not recall any problems with the curriculum during her beginning years. She enjoyed the planning. "The curriculum was not the issue. It was how *hard the work* was!"

CONCLUSION

While it is easy for policy makers and politicians to call for PDS work, actually doing PDS work is not easy. Conflicting ideas about what constitutes good teacher preparation and the purpose of the partnership plagued the PDS from its beginning. The elementary school partnership was characterized by lurching forward around loosely articulated points of consensus and faltering as various participants interpreted them with gradations of meaning. While Kay was "oblivious" to the political nuances in the beginning, they were part of the context that shaped her student teaching and, at least in part, account for the internship failing to provide her with more than an enriched student-teaching experience.

The professional norm that surrounded her was characterized by ideas in conflict, uncertainty, ambiguity, and constant adjustment of practice. In such an environment teaching is absorbing. There is always more to learn. And nobody knows all the secrets of success. The essential ingredient—a professional learning environment—is not uniformity of practice or absence of conflict, but the commitment of a professional community to move forward amid conflict, uncertainty, ambiguity, and constant adjustment. In such an environment a neophyte teacher is not expected to know everything because it is clear that mature professionals do not know all there is to know. A professional is expected to question, debate, experiment, and keep coming to the table to talk about differences. A professional is not expected to replicate one best way of doing things, but to experiment with multiple ways of doing. In such an environment every child has a chance to learn because no professional will give up because the known and expected solutions do not work.

Significantly, Kay was not abandoned at any point in her early development. While the feedback and support may not have been perfect, it was available. During her student teaching she had cooperating teachers, college supervisors, and peers who were able to talk to her about issues of practice and help her to think through what she wanted and needed from teaching. Being in the classroom and at the university simultaneously immersed her in practice while enabling her to withdraw and reflect on the experience through her reflective journal and course content. Specific assignments, such as the child study projects and the school study, introduced second semester, helped her to see children and the learning environment in new ways. Just as the child study opened her eyes to new ways of seeing a child, so did the school study second semester broaden Kay's vision of the school. (The school study is discussed in more detail in Chapter 7.)

While her cooperating teachers were collaborative, other student teachers had different experiences. Kay noted:

It really made me realize how many different styles and opinions and methods are going on in one school. Two students attending a school can get completely different learning experiences depending on their teachers, friends, and attitudes. As a teacher you can really make your experience different by associating with different staff members.

The internship, with all its faults, allowed Kay to work closely with two very different professionals and contrast her own ideas with theirs. And her beginning year was in a familiar context with support from her mentor and the opportunity to collaborate with colleagues. Such an environment was "good enough" to stimulate and support Kay's reconstruction of personal knowledge.

ഇ 6 ൭

Revisiting the Barriers to Teaching

> There are definitely moments when I am at a loss for what
> to do, but I now know I have the tools within me to figure
> out the next step.
>
> —Kay, 1994

INITIALLY, I DESCRIBED Kay as someone at risk. In order to have a successful career as a teacher, Kay had to "beat the odds" against her dropping out at the end of her preparation program or within the first 5 years of her career. We examined a number of barriers that stand between promising, academically able teacher prospects and a career in teaching. These barriers included her own preconceptions and implicit theories about teaching and learning, the separation of theory and practice, the concern for control, and the incompatibility of reflective practice with schools.

In this chapter, we return to these barriers to Kay's future as a deliberative teacher and examine them in light of her successful career. In doing so, we also see how her nascent inclinations about teaching—classroom environments should nurture active learning, learning should be fun, teachers should have an experimental attitude, and teachers should be sensitive to the social context of schooling—have become an enduring part of Kay's makeup as a teacher. But first, we will take a look at Kay in action and the classroom environment she has created.

KAY IN ACTION

Even though the PDS had set standards for the supervision of student teachers and interns that required cooperating teachers to have a minimum of 2 years of classroom experience, the standards did not apply to other colleges that used the PDS as a placement site for teacher preparation. In fact, the active parent association made an effort to get student teachers in every classroom, seeing them as a key to providing individualized attention to children.

While Kay was an intern, she shared her classroom with a TC student teacher, Hannah, who was assigned to Susan and Ellie. In her first year as a teacher, she was given a student teacher from another college. As Kay recalls:

> I had them almost from day 1. The year I was interning, as I was taking over, Hannah was there as the student teacher, and I think we had somebody else also. So they were there from that first year, and I believe the next year I had one. You know I never made the conscious decision of having them or not having them, they were always there. . . . But I think with Hannah, it was good to have her there, and she was pretty strong as far as teaching was concerned, and we got along really well, but I did let Susan do most of the mentoring. We were more—sort of like [she pauses] you know, peers.

Kay's former student teachers and interns provide a rich source of insight about her as a teacher through their descriptions of her in their reflective journals and interviews with them in their beginning years as teachers. Khristine, who was Kay's first TC student teacher, was an intern in the newly revised PDS program. She was assigned to Kay in January of her second year as a teacher. Jessie interned during Kay's third year as a teacher, Candice in year 4, and Brenda student-taught with her in year 5. I draw on their perspectives as well as my own hours in Kay's classroom—many with student teachers, since I supervised them all, with the exception of Khristine.

The Classroom Environment

The terms *order* and *activity* best describe Kay's classroom. This can be illustrated by an excerpt from Jessie's student-teaching journal, written the first day of school in a second-grade classroom, during Kay's third year as a teacher:

> The children have just arrived. Kay greets them at the door and explains that they will find a schedule written on the chalkboard. It begins with an activity, "Do Now." She explains that they will be making a balloon with their names on it to go on the door so everybody will know who is in the room and decorating a label to go on their mailboxes. She gives directions about finding a place at

one of the tables. The children enter the room, scrambling for
chairs.

Kay's schedule covers the full schoolday:

SCHEDULE

Do Now	Balloons for door. Decorate/name. Labels for mailbox.
Meeting	On rug
10:20	Yard
	Lunchroom practice
	Math—"Just to get us thinking about math again"
12:15	Lunch—Jessie stays full day
1:00	Silent reading—Jessie reads with Timmy and Cass
	Scavenger hunt
	Clean-up
	Read aloud
3:15	Dismissal

In addition to the schedule, Kay typically has a chart for classroom jobs
and an organizer for bathroom. These, too, are written on the chalkboard.
There is little space on the chalkboard for anything like a traditional
"chalk and talk" lesson. Only a small space of the board is reserved for
writing. To one side of the chalkboard is a large rug marking off the
meeting area. A flip chart with newsprint pad stands nearby. Kay uses
paper to record the children's ideas. Within a few days the chalkboard
is covered with these chart papers. The meeting area also serves as a
library, with bookshelves lining a wall shelf under windows that stretch
along one side of the room. Books are color-coded with dots to indicate
category—orange = poetry, green = picture, red = beginning chapter
books, yellow = harder chapter books, and the like. Books are about children from various cultural backgrounds. A table and shelves with more
storage for supplies border the rug area. All supplies are held in common.
   The desks occupy the front part of the classroom, bordering the carpet
on one side. They are arranged in banks of four or six. Each bank holds
a magazine box with five folders per student, color-coded. The closet
space along one wall has a mailbox and coat hook for each child. Along
the back wall are more bulletin boards and a round table and chairs. As
Brenda recalls, Kay's desk is "a junk collector . . . set up in the corner as
a private space, but she didn't really sit there." She uses the file cabinet
for her personal things. A sink, easel, and more storage complete the
circumference of the room. The room is well ordered, and children can

see at a glance where everything is to be found. The effect is an environment that is bright, colorful, and seems to belong to the children.

Children talk with each other while they work on their balloon labels. Candice recalls that there is always a "Do Now":

> It's just something that when the kids come in—kids straggle in at different times—they can do by the time it's about 9:00 A.M. They are done. And they can talk and it isn't a mind drainer . . . a focuser, yet the kids can chat. It is either an introduction to a topic, or it's a review so sometimes she realizes they haven't been doing well on, like, addition. She'll slip in a couple of [problems]. They usually are fun, very few are not. They are just kind of gameish . . . a warm-up.

Jessie notes in her journal that as children work on their "Do Now" balloons on that first day:

> The social interaction seemed to be just as significant as the task. Some children (most?) talked with their neighbors and kept an eye on what others were drawing or writing. . . . I noticed that some children sort of looked out of the corner of their eye to see if they were being watched by the teacher, especially when they were whispering to their neighbors.

As they become more socialized to the room and each other, they "share materials, help answer questions, and in general cooperate and also engage in cooperative learning. For the most part the groups are small and well matched so that hardly anyone is left out," Candice writes.

By the end of the week the bulletin boards and wall space are also covered with chart paper posters generated from math, language, and social studies work. Jessie notices how the balloons, which children made during their "Do Now" exercise the first day, appear on the door and their decorative labels mark the mailboxes Kay has arranged for them using cardboard containers. In their descriptions of the classroom environment, Kay's student teachers consistently comment on the detailed organization of the classroom. Candice describes Kay's classroom as

> extremely structured, extremely structured. For as free as it seems and as much rein as the kids have, there is a time and a place for everything. And the subs that come into the classroom are just in awe because it is so organized. And yet it is not uncomfortable or sterile. She painted everything aqua—all the desks. They didn't

match and they were driving her crazy. All the bookshelves are this aqua color, so it is very bright and extremely organized. Everything is in its place.

Brenda describes the overall effect as "very uncluttered and comfortable and it didn't seem confining . . . the children could move around in it."

A Commanding Presence

Kay seems to be everywhere at once during children's work periods. Today is typical. I've charted her movement during a 20-minute period at times, only to find my field notes a tangled maze of lines and time notations. Typically, she interacts with each group and with each child before a period is over, fields questions from around the room, and is alert to potential problems or interruptions. It is a rare work period when she does not get to every child at least once, spending anywhere from a few seconds to several minutes with groups, focusing on each individual through comments, gestures, or eye contact. She positions herself at eye level when she speaks to a child, either by squatting down next to the table or leaning over. More often than not, she is questioning rather than giving directions.

When it is time to go to the rug for meeting, Kay asks for attention. Her voice reaches the far corners of the room—she could have been on stage, she has a voice that carries. She asks the children to take their supplies to the "back rug," giving them a specific place to put them—she says this keeps them from bombarding her with things to put away and gives them ownership of the classroom.

While Kay's manner with children during the work time is quiet, she has a commanding presence. When she speaks, her voice carries above the children's activity, however loud. Jessie is troubled by this at first. "I still can't believe how noisy and fidgety these kids are. And Kay's normal voice is so loud and commanding that she can talk over everyone so there is no need for them to be quiet." Initially, Khristine sees it as harsh and threatening:

I'm very surprised at Kay's harsh tone with many of the children. I am unaccustomed to threats like "You will benched if you . . . " or "I'm taking time away from your choice time if you don't . . . " —I wonder if such threats actually work.

On one occasion, early in her semester with Kay, Jessie spoke to me about her concern. I suggested that she do a content analysis of Kay's comments and notice how children seem to react to them. Jessie was surprised at the result because Kay did not actually seem to be threatening. As student teachers adjust to her personality and demeanor, they see her tone of voice in a new light. Candice explains that Kay's voice

> fills the room, but it is not yelling. It is kind of interesting. She really, really projects like from the diaphragm and you can hear it everywhere . . . on a field trip you could hear her from one end of the subway car to the other end. She was just like that . . . and she has eyes in the back of her head like most teachers, and she has the voice like, "*RICKY!*" She has a very powerful voice. She is very conscious of it. . . . She said to me, "You can, you should come up with some different classroom management strategies because I have a loud voice so I can do this, but you have got more of a soft demeanor."

Candice recalls that when Kay uses her voice to discipline a child or the class, she is more likely to become quiet than to yell. When she gets very, very quiet, the children take notice.

While Jessie wrestles with the issue of voice, she notes only one instance in which Kay actually yells at the children. Two boys are fighting for a spot in the front of the line as they prepare to leave the yard. One pushes, and a fight begins. Kay is at the back of the line. "She had had it. I guess she screamed at [them] for a few minutes."

Jessie begins to notice, however, that the usual pattern for discipline is through the curriculum. Kay pulls children to the rug to give directions rather than talking with them while they are at their desks. She focuses them on learning tasks and encourages them to settle the problems they have in working together before she intervenes. She uses language like "you need" and "these are the choices." Her directions are concrete and sequential. Kay's classes are always lively, and she has a high tolerance for noise if the children are on task.

Negotiables and Non-Negotiables

Candice describes "three non-negotiables that go on every day." One is the Do Now, another is silent reading for half an hour after lunch, and the third is the read aloud at the end of the day. The silent reading and read aloud are very relaxed for students— "they can lay on the floor." Kay "usually tries to do math or reading right after the Do Now because they need the most energy or whatever and then does the opposite every other day." Candice giggles as she recalls how much math *she* learned from Kay!

There are variations to the pattern:

> Oh, Monday there isn't a Do Now. It is a spelling pretest, and she does do spelling traditionally. She does let them do inventive spelling in their own writing, but when it is published, [their writing must have correct] spelling. At the same time every week she gives them a new group of words, so once they've learned them and taken the [final] test, they are responsible from then on for those words. So that is also an underlying structure. Sometimes she does science in the morning, sometimes in the afternoon. And social studies is, a lot of the time, [integrated into] literature, math, science. Sometimes it is a thing unto itself; it kind of depends on what the topic is. Sometimes social studies takes over 2 hours of the day just because . . . she has no set time, like sometimes math could be 15 minutes or 1½ hours. It just depends on how long she feels it will take.

So, while the underlying structure may not vary—math every morning, for example—the amount of time actually spent on an activity will vary depending on the task.

Candice points out that the time is preplanned, and "she usually gets it pretty close once she knows the kids." She "gives a bunch of assessments" and knows where they are and what she wants them to do; and she plans. "It is something she said she was very aware of because when she first started teaching she was very off in time and late to everything or too early."

Sensitivity to Needs

Not only do Kay's student teachers see her as highly organized, but they also talk about her sensitivity to the needs of children (including their cultural backgrounds). Jessie notices, in the first day described above, that Kay seems to be very aware of the children's feelings. She comments, "During the meeting there were so many questions. It seemed necessary to spend time answering quite a few—almost as though it lessened some 'pressure' or anxiety for each child." Later, Jessie observes that when she introduces the math activity, Kay tells children it is as a way to find out "what you've done before and what you haven't." Nobody has to feel badly about not being able to do any of the problems.

Candice recalls that Kay is aware when children get tired, "which my grade school teachers never seemed to know." She does not hesitate to stop and say to the children, "You know, this isn't working, we'll come back to it tomorrow." Even though she has a time for everything, she is not a slave to the time. "She will never just drag something on until lunch," Candice quips.

Kay's flexibility and willingness to try new things, her fairness, involvement of parents, understanding of curriculum, and manner of supporting them as student teachers are consistently noticed and commented on by her student teachers. They feel lucky to have her as their cooperating teacher. Khristine writes in her student-teaching journal, "As much as I am a self-reflective person, and as much as I want to grow and improve as a teacher, I do dread hearing negative things. Kay had a few suggestions, but she said them in such a way that I felt good about myself and my teaching."

At the end of a hard day in which she has not felt successful, Candice writes, "Kay was very cool. She sort of nonchalantly mentioned stuff I left out without making me self-conscious or the children suspicious of my ability."

On one occasion Jessie has an idea about how to rearrange the desks. Kay says they can try, so they move all the furniture around. In the end, they go back to the way things were, but Jessie notes it in her journal as "a perfect example of Kay's attitude. She is totally open to trying new ideas. This openness and flexibility has been so helpful to me." Jessie feels like "an integral and valued part of the classroom" and hopes she will be able to maintain the relationship once the semester is over.

The children in her classroom seem to like coming to school. For the most part, parents like having their children with Kay, often commenting on how much they are learning. Kay has a high level of parent involvement in the classroom and is constantly soliciting their participation, particularly in social studies. At the beginning of the year she collects information from parents. Candice remembers that Kay asked them to write a letter about their child, telling the child's interests, hopes, fears, and the like. She is respectful of parents, too. Candice recalls that even when Kay was very concerned about how parents were dealing with an issue, "she was always on the level like, 'We need to talk.'" She would be very direct, "I am concerned about your child. You're the parent and it's your decision, but here's what I think." Kay never came across as, "I'm the teacher and I know all."

Kay, as teacher, is in the process of inventing herself in the role. She is not the teacher of her early school recollections. Nor is she some idealized version of a constructivist teacher. She is a successful teacher, somewhere between the two—more constructivist than traditional. With this in mind, we look at her again in light of the barriers she had to overcome to succeed in teaching. The first of these has to do with her prior knowledge of teaching.

PAST THE PRECONCEPTIONS HURDLE

In previous chapters, I have paid a great deal of attention to teachers' preconceptions and implicit theories through examining teachers' early recollections. I have argued that teacher-preparation and staff development programs should foster a healthy deconstruction/reconstruction of personal knowledge rather than attempting to replace it with official teacher education knowledge. The process of deconstruction and reconstruction takes time. In looking at Kay's development as a student teacher, we have already identified tensions between her own success as a student in traditional classrooms and her inclination toward constructivist theory and practice. The tensions have not been resolved as a result of the TC program but continue to present themselves in her early years as a teacher. As years pass, we find Kay to be someone who has reconstructed but not replaced prior experiences. She is probably much more conscious of her prior experiences than she was as a teacher education student. She has searched for a balance in classroom life that is right for her, and the search will probably continue throughout her career.

Finding the Right Balance

By the end of her fifth year of teaching Kay has arrived at a teaching style that seems authentically her own. She sees herself as a blend of progressive and traditional approaches.

> The ways that I group the kids and have them work together is definitely progressive. It isn't traditional. They don't sit in rows, they don't even sit at desks, but all work is meant for them to do together with an occasional, "This is something you need to do on your own." The give-and-take and the structure built in for give-and-take about peer-editing conferences and choosing roles, picking your strengths, and all of that is the progressive side. The traditional side is some of the routines of the classroom, I think. When we're having a discussion, it's still hard for me to just let everybody freely talk. So your hand has to be raised. And certainly we can go back and forth. . . . When we line up, we're still in two

lines—all of that is a school thing anyway. But the routine stuff is more on the traditional side, whereas the teaching might not be. The math is both—lots of games and lots of problem solving. But memorizing the times table comes in!

Candice recalls making a comment to Kay about being progressive. Kay said "she is progressive but not that progressive."

Kay's desire for school to be fun and her experience of a traditional approach to teaching as fun have been tempered by her growing understanding of curriculum, teaching and learning, and her own needs. Kay talks about her need for the structure and routine that are hallmarks of her classroom:

> There is a definite routine in my classroom. I need [routines] to function. I very honestly think that about half the kids need them to function. Some kids are fine without them. But some need them to get through the day, and I need them to get through the day. There is a time when math is taught. There is a place to put this paper and pencil. It is the routines of the classroom that are more set.

Building a Cooperative Approach

Kay's way of working within the organizational framework is heavily dependent on cooperative learning and children's interests. It has been influenced by her preparation in cooperative learning, group process, child study, and experiences as a student teacher, intern, and teacher. She recalls learning how to conduct "the group discussions we do so much of in my social studies or literature groups." Even though she participated in a reading group as a child, group discussion and cooperative learning were not a part of her childhood experience. But it is likely that her satisfaction with having children work in groups connects to the beliefs about teaching that are summarized by her early memory of getting to go to a special table with other children to read. And we can conjecture, without too great a stretch of the imagination, that her desire to have tables rather than desks is connected to her childhood feelings of being at a table.

Putting the children together at tables and asking them to work together does not necessarily result in real democratic, cooperative learning, and Kay is aware that it has taken her years to develop authentic group discussions. It is an ideal that she still works toward. Typically, Kay sets up an activity, perhaps giving a mini-lesson. Then children have a task to do, perhaps a worksheet or a project. For example, weighing and measuring pumpkins of different sizes using standard and nonstandard measures was an activity I observed one day. Each child has a worksheet with places to record information. Pumpkins and various equipment for weight and measurement are at each table. Kay has children identify the equipment at their table and its use. She elicits some inventive ways in which they might weigh and measure. Then she has children work together. It is noisy as they consult and record the information. In some instances, children work in the group but seem to pay little attention to the group. Kay moves from table to table asking task questions—"What is the first thing you should be doing?"—and focusing questions—"What would happen if you did it another way?"

In Brenda's opinion, children do not really cooperate in Kay's classroom. "A lot of the work wasn't true cooperative learning in that they worked individually in groups." When Kay reflects on her early efforts to develop collaboration among children, she realizes that often there were collections of individuals working in the same place rather than real conversations around tasks. But anyone spending time in her classroom will admit that the whole environment is set up for collaboration.

Candice differentiates between cooperation and cooperative learning, a distinction that many student teachers miss:

> Students in my class both cooperate and do cooperative learning. They share materials, help answer questions, and in general cooperate—and they also engage in cooperative learning. For the most part groups are small and well matched so that hardly anyone is left out. The most recent example of cooperative learning was a discussion and list making of "What is an American?" Each table engaged in a lively discussion and created original and varied lists.

Like most student teachers who are trying out a cooperative learning model, Brenda wants it to be perfect, as indicated by her earlier comment. Kay seems more content to move gradually toward the behavior she desires from children than her student teachers are. Jessie's experience in getting children to collaborate on a Do Now is an example of how Kay sees the possibilities despite the imperfections that occur in execution.

Jessie has put together a Do Now involving a word-problems activity. She gives an explanation out in the hallway, as Kay often does, but realizes that she has not been as clear as she needed to be once they begin. The children are supposed to work together on all the problems and come up with an explanation for how they did each. Every group is to identify one of these problems and explain how they solved it to the whole class.

The activity is difficult and requires a great deal of coaching from Jessie and Kay. Jessie feels stressed by the noise and chaos. Kay suggests that the activity is important enough to extend the time for Do Now. "She felt that learning to work as a group was very important and that we should continue until we finished." In the end, and despite Jessie's nervousness at running overtime, all of the groups come to consensus and offer an explanation using the chalkboard and verbal descriptions. "The fact that they did accomplish it with all the confusion and noise and challenge means in some ways it was a success," Jessie says.

Reframing Bad Experiences

Collaborative approaches to learning are appealing to Kay because she thinks they are more fun for children and they end up learning more through interacting with each other and discovery. Kay's implicit theory—that learning should be fun—was confirmed through countless school experiences in which she enjoyed herself, and she wants children to enjoy themselves. But she remembers other experiences in which learning was *not* fun. These, too, have fed her implicit theory. In deconstructing her prior experiences, Kay becomes conscious of how the contrast between negative experiences she had in social studies and the way she has learned to teach social studies plays out in her own classroom.

> I remember in sixth grade, sitting there in social studies learning about religions of the world through a textbook and literally not understanding a word I was reading, but reading it and answering the questions like I had to and to this day not remembering a single thing that I learned in that class. I definitely keep remembering those things when I think about how I'm going to teach something. I know reading and answering the questions is not going to teach . . . what you need to teach.

Kay's social studies curriculum and her classroom environment challenge the traditional "textbook" knowledge with which she was reared. She uses multiple resources, including books, artifacts, and people. Her student teachers notice that classroom bookshelves are full of multicultural books, although Candice is concerned that there are not as many good books about Hispanic children. They notice that she is respectful of cultural traditions. She is careful to help children see indigenous people in a positive light in studies of the history of Manhattan and Puerto Rico. She wants them to examine events from perspectives of the various people involved in them. She wants children to recognize that others, who have understood them differently, often contest our understanding of the same events.

Kay likes to get parents involved when she can. When she teaches a unit around a theme—Manhattan neighborhoods, for example—she elicits participation from parents and builds on the children's own cultural traditions.

Student teachers are encouraged to bring their own traditions into the classroom, too. Candice delights in being able to suggest and teach a unit on *Dia de los Muetros*, or Day of the Dead, one of Mexico's traditional holidays honoring beloved ancestors, family, and friends. Even though Kay is somewhat adamant in her dislike of holidays in the curriculum, she supports Candice. Candice is particularly pleased when Kay joins in the fun and writes a lengthy entry in her journal about how Kay has explained to a child that she cannot make ghosts or vampires instead of a skull because ghosts and vampires are not a part of the cultural tradition of *Dia de los Muetros*.

Blending Traditional and Progressive Approaches

Two contrasting activities show how Kay uses both progressive and traditional methods, as a result of the reconstructive process that has occurred in her teaching journey. The first is a food fest that children have planned following completion of their books in literature groups. Khristine reports that each group prepares something based on their book; for example, one group "concocted a wonderful mixture of juices. . . . Then Kay gathered the children in the meeting area to discuss all the different ways we used math in the preparations and how the food related to each literature group." Kay has thoroughly integrated literature, social studies, and mathematics in the culminating activity.

At the same time, Khristine notices that Kay spends time getting their third-graders ready for state examinations:

> We'd both like to have the children engage in rather extensive manipulative work but are hurried by the demands of the state. Underlying the whole dilemma is Kay's feeling that she owes it to the children to at least introduce them to the concepts covered on the test. Having them sit for an exam on concepts with which they've had no contact would frustrate them.

On another day Khristine remarks:

> The children spent most of the morning working on math exam practice books and reading exam practice books. . . . The upcoming

citywide exam is beginning to bother me because having the children do practice exams makes me realize how unfair standardized tests really are.

Kay attends to the "traditional" curriculum by giving children direct practice in exam taking, but is very child centered in her keen awareness of their feelings. Following the exam, Khristine reports:

> We let the children talk and socialize for about 15 minutes and then gathered them into the meeting area. Kay followed up on Monday's conversation about the exam and asked them what they thought about it now that it was over. Most of the children said they thought they did fine and that they felt well prepared. We gave them treats Kay and I had brought in for the occasion.

Kay reflects on the pressure that tests exert on the curriculum:

> I really hate it. And actually, that's one of the reasons I'm really pushing to move down to second grade, because getting these third-graders ready for four state tests is just . . . obnoxious. So it does ruin—and we do do test preparation—they don't know how to take a test. I mean, especially in this school, they've barely even taken a spelling quiz, you know. I'm not saying whether that's bad or good, but the fact that all of a sudden they have to sit down and take a 2-hour test, you know, that's like . . . so we do a lot of test preparation.

Kay is keenly aware that her curriculum and teaching reflect past as well as teacher-preparation experiences. For example, she usually teaches spelling traditionally, following a spelling textbook. On Mondays the children have a pretest of their words. They may also choose some additional words from their written work so that lists are personalized. They are expected to study these words, complete spelling exercises, and take a test. But, as mentioned earlier, inventive spelling is encouraged in writing assignments at the draft stage. She identifies the way she teaches spelling as directly connecting to one of her most unpleasant memories of school:

> Because you can't spell or because your handwriting is messy does not make you an unintelligent child or person. I could not spell. I spell better today, but it is definitely a deficit of mine. As a kid, it was brought up *constantly*. Like, "You need to rewrite because it is spelled wrong. You need to take this spelling test over." I had to take the spelling test home to my parents because I got more

wrong than you were allowed to. It wasn't from not studying. I just do not have a mind for spelling. I remember that in elementary school—I don't remember it so much once I got to junior high and high school—it being *such a factor* in my education. Part of it was that I know my parents would tell the teacher, "Don't accept it if it's not spelled right," that was part of their mindset as well.

Kay has taken her negative experiences and allowed them to teach her to do the opposite.

As a teacher what I've realized is that you can't look at a paper, then judge a child's writing based on the grammar or the structure of it: the spelling of it, the handwriting of it. You've got to take it as a whole, and certainly work with the kids on the areas that they're [deficient] in. But I also really think there isn't any one way to teach spelling. There are better ways and worse ways, but berating kids for it and telling them, "You're not studying enough," is not the way to get them to do it.

Kay still wants to teach in ways that are fun for the children. Khristine remembers a measurement unit that Kay needed to teach in a short period of time. Her solution was to divide the unit into four sessions. There were two student teachers, so Kay asked each to come up with a game to teach one of the sessions. They ran simultaneously, covering the material in ways that were interesting to the children.

In thinking about her own practice, now that she is a veteran teacher, Kay comments:

What I strive for, ideally, is to be casual, yet still have that structure that I wanted to have. The conversations and the interplay between us is casual, not formal, it's very comfortable. . . . I just want the general feel to be much more comfortable, but still being able to get it together when they have to. My ideal would be that they know when conversations should be happening and when let's just do the traditional kind of listen.

CONCLUSION

Kay's inclination to experiment along with her strong belief that learning should be fun—both apparent in her practice, and now well developed in her thinking about teaching—were not implanted by her preservice program. Rather, they were inclinations, part of her own cultural history, that were supported and developed by the program and have evolved over her years of teaching. Britzman (1986) suggests that being situated within one's own history is empowering. By becoming participants in their own development, teachers will be moved beyond the sway of cultural authority. She acknowledges that this can be a difficult and painful experience in that although experiences of being in schools and classrooms are familiar, the experience of being teacher is not familiar to neophyte teachers.

Disequilibrium created by discontinuity between past and present is necessary for transformation to occur. Becoming self-critical requires more than being in the classroom. It requires deliberate attention to developing an understanding of school and classroom context and culture. Britzman (1986) argues that without such understanding neophyte teachers are likely to be trapped in a cycle of cultural maintenance and reproduction.

Kay's preparation challenged her to examine her own preconceptions through a variety of reflective activities. The reconstruction process was supported, but it was nevertheless a conflicted process, full of tension. Like most student teachers in the program, Kay did not miss the emphasis on reflection. Kay has rethought her experiences and surfaced many of her implicit theories, enlarging and deepening her understanding of what she already knew. Her preparation program began a process that, once well launched, has stayed with her:

> I often find myself saying, "Well, they're just not ready for that yet," or "I really think they're ready for that, lets do that," you know, that kind of outlook. Then there's an emotional side to it . . . sometimes when parents say, "Well, why are you spending so much time . . . " I don't know, studying about China or whatever it is, and I'm like, "Well, it's because it's something they enjoy and they're learning how to learn through that," so that emotional factor: if they're enjoying it and it's a means for getting to where we need to be. So I find myself justifying myself that way, too, "Well this is getting them interested," and then through that they will still learn what they need to learn.
>
> I think comparing my education to theirs—I see how worthwhile it is. It's how much they go home talking about China, or they go home talking about fractions, or whatever it is, whereas I didn't do that, I mean I cringed when my parents said, "Let's go to a museum because there is something connected to what you

are studying in school," I mean *if* I ever even went home and told them what I was studying in school. I don't think I did.

Kay has been able to develop a constant dialectic between the present moment as she sees it, her own biography, and theories of teaching and learning—a critical stance toward teaching. Developing the ability to examine preconceptions and implicit theories—personal knowledge—and to raise questions about one's own actions is critical if teachers are to overcome the other barriers to the profession. In the following chapter we explore each of these barriers in greater depth, noting how her own reconstruction of theoretical and practical knowledge fosters a critical, reflective process that has contributed to her staying on in teaching.

❧ 7 ☙

A Constant and Consistent Dialectic

I guess I stayed in teaching because I was always learning. I
always wanted to know more. There never was a time when
I felt like something couldn't be done.

— Kay, 2001

THE UNNATURAL SEPARATION of theory from practice, the struggle for
control of the classroom, and the incompatibility of reflective practice
with goals of schools are all negative dynamics identified in the literature
on teaching. Initially, we looked at each of these as barriers to Kay's future
in teaching as an academically able teacher education student. Admittedly,
Kay could spend years in schools without concerning herself with whether
or not she is being affected by such dynamics. She could "forget everything they tried to teach you in the ivory tower," as one of my colleagues
advised me in my early years of elementary school teaching. Many teachers do. Or she could adopt the attitude of another of my colleagues along
the way, who explained, "I've seen ideas come and go. They're all the
same in the end. I've found out what works, and I do it." What worked
for her was a file cabinet full of aging worksheet duplication masters.
The pessimistic advice of my well-intended colleagues is not so unusual.
But Kay's teacher-preparation program was designed to contradict and
overcome such pessimism and offer her a more hopeful outlook on the
profession.

In this chapter, we look at Kay's practical theory in use. We also see
how she has dealt with the issue of control—already broached in the
discussion of how student teachers experienced her "commanding" voice.
And we see how she continues to reflect on her teaching in the context
of an urban school.

PAST THE THEORY–PRACTICE BARRIER

Kay's student-teaching placement, internship, and subsequent career at
a PDS placed her in a context where the theory–practice debate was live-

ly and ongoing, as we noted in Chapter 5. Britzman (1986) comments that during student teaching educational theory should begin to inform practice as "the metamorphosis from the role of student to that of teacher" begins (p. 442). But the predominant model of teacher education is consistent with what most people believe: Universities invent new knowledge in the form of theory, and practical life goes on elsewhere.

There was an unconscious buy-in to this way of thinking by most of the key players in the PDS. In this way of thinking, learning theory in teacher education is more or less a rite of passage, but it is of little practical use except as the student teacher is able to integrate the two worlds of university and school, usually in the form of fresh new methods or tips on teaching. This is a technical orientation to teaching and learning that emphasizes teacher training over teacher education and has little to do with the social and political realities of schooling. Indeed, if teaching can be isolated into acts of teaching to be learned and practiced, then we might presume that these acts of teaching are culturally neutral (Schoonmaker, 2001). The predominant model of teacher education actually feeds into the notion that teacher preparation ought to be removed from universities and placed in the hands of school people who know something about how to teach and what children really need.

Furthermore, this pattern of thinking has tended to separate the teacher from the intellectual life of teaching and the process of curriculum development from that of instruction (Schoonmaker, 2001). That is, curriculum development, or the intellectual work of theorizing, is left to off-site experts, while teachers are left with the role of putting the ideas of curriculum developers into practice. Their task is not a curricular task, but one of implementation of the curriculum, or instruction. The separation of curriculum and teaching has been apparent not only in various "teacher-proof" curriculum models but also in staff development models that prepare teachers to focus on their instructional behaviors without questioning whether the curriculum they are teaching is worthwhile.

Paulo Freire (1970/1999) spoke of praxis as reflective or thoughtful action. For Freire, praxis stands between intellectualism, or reflection without action, and activism, or action without reflection. James Macdonald (1975) argued that curriculum development should be seen as praxis, but he did not connect curriculum development with implementation, falling short of real praxis. It is at the juncture between the intended curriculum and the curriculum in use that the teacher stands. When the teacher focuses on teaching practice as the skillful delivery and management of a curriculum, he or she is engaged in activism. The real place of theory in a practical profession is in bridging the intellectual work of theorizing about learning and what is to be learned and the real people in the classroom with their own interests, wishes, and needs. Instruction is not a manipulative process in which the teacher uses motivational psychology to get students to behave themselves and to learn things that may not be worth learning, but a dynamic process in which the teacher's own theoretical constructs play a part (see Bolin, 1987).

Teaching as Theory in Use

Kay encountered and circumvented the theory–practice barrier in several significant ways. Her preservice program had emphasized the role of teacher as deliberative curriculum decision maker, equipping student teachers with skills of curriculum design and assessment. This perspective assumes that all *acts of teaching* are based on some theoretical conception of teaching and learning, however nascent or unarticulated it may be. What the teacher chooses to encourage, ignore, elicit, or even forbid will be based on more or less systematic ideas about how children learn, what they need, and what is worth knowing and doing. Kay was equipped to be a student of teaching and of children and to maintain an experimental attitude toward her work. This is akin to what Marilyn Cochran-Smith and Susan L. Lytle (2001) refer to as "knowledge of practice" and "inquiry as stance," arguing that the worlds of formal and practical knowledge cannot be divided for professional development. They argue that teachers should "generate local knowledge *of* practice by working within the contexts of inquiry communities to theorize and construct their work and to connect it to larger social, cultural, and political issues" (p. 48).

A sophisticated integration of Kay's program and the daily work of teaching did not happen all at once, but it did happen. As Brenda, who taught with her during the spring semester of Kay's fifth year as a teacher, recalls, "She said it took like 5 years before she really felt everything she learned clicked into place." Kay tells her, "Everything you learn in the program catches up with you eventually and then you realize why you learned it and why you are taught it. But it takes a while."

Kay tries to help student teachers see how their preservice program will work for them over time as they become more skillful in studying children and context and in designing curriculum. "I guess that they don't quite feel like that they have the practical part of it." She recalls having the same feelings.

Working from Children's Interests

Student teachers recognize that Kay's theory in use is child centered. "It is very simple. We work from their experiences," Brenda explains. Khristine recalls:

I could see elements of different educators, bigger educators than her . . . we talked about why she did things certain ways . . . right before the [math] tests. . . . She would say, "I'm throwing educa-tion theory aside. I need to make sure they know what a foot or inch is . . . this is not my usual way of doing this . . . my theory of education is this but I've got to just burst this through."

This was a conscious departure for Kay, who preferred to get the chil-dren involved in "using theories and making theories about probability themselves and other things," as Brenda notices.

Khristine remembers that Kay modeled theoretical commitments that she did not necessarily talk about. "She didn't say, 'Well every time I start a discussion I try to figure out what the kids know and then based on that I make decisions about what to do next.' She very rarely said that." Looking back on it, Khristine sees "that's what she was doing."

Kay's nascent theory—that children will learn best if it is fun—has blossomed into a way of being in the classroom. Not only does she rely on games and manipulatives in teaching math; the social studies pro-gram is also inquiry-based. Khristine remembers:

She really believed in, like, letting them do it. And there were cer-tain kids who weren't doing it at all and I was, as a student teacher you're always aware of who is not doing what they are ex-pected to do versus as a teacher you're working with the kids who are. Five or six kids are just sloughing off, but she was always aware that they were and then working with them individually to kind of get them up to speed.

Kay is demanding, she expects a lot of the children, but she does not give meaningless homework. She is process oriented as well as interested in high academic results. The academic program can be fun, and it is given depth and breadth because Kay is a keen observer of children and a continuous student of teaching.

Continuous Learning

Candice remembers what happened when Kay took a course on the learning environment at TC. It strengthened what was already a strong commitment to cooperative learning and helped her to refine the way she worked with cooperative groups. It also reinforced her commitment to working from the needs and interests of children. All the time that she was taking the course, she was applying the principles she was learning to her classroom. She wondered about whether it was "kids' space" or "teacher's space" and confessed to a certain amount of guilt over having a teacher-sized chair in the room. As she reflected on the course content, Kay referred to her preservice experience and how it related. She was always coming up with books that had influenced her and that she thought Candice might find useful.

Kay believes that her child study project, during student teaching, got her to think about learning theory and child development as a neophyte teacher. She never forgot what she learned from the project, both the skills in observation and the emotional impact of looking closely at one child over time.

> She was a real difficult child, I don't know why I picked this challenging child, I remember she barely spoke. I definitely started to think, "How can I help this person?" and lean back on what I'd read, . . . which I did a lot more consciously than I would do now. I mean now it's a lot more subconscious I'm sure and also because it's not a one on one. I mean I do, I sit there and think, "Oh, Alex really needs some help, how can I help her," but it's not as focused on . . . one child.

Lesson planning and curriculum development were also ways that Kay recalls connecting theory and practice. She was required to think about appropriate assessment at the end of each lesson plan—"I remember that being tough for me at first." By having to think about how she would know whether students were learning, Kay had to examine her own understanding of teaching and learning. While there was considerable debate about the nature of the TC program and whether or not it was "too theoretical," Kay never really separated the two. "Theory to me is a way of doing something . . . a path . . . somebody decided, 'This is the way it should be.' . . . that written path is the theory." For Kay, theory is the path, and practice is walking on the path.

Very early in her experience, she began formulating her own theories and testing them—in effect, walking on her own path. In doing so, she is using what John Elliott has called *practical* theory (1976–77). According to Grierson (1974), practical theory may be seen as the application of common sense to human action and interpretation of meaning in the everyday world. Commonsense knowing "provides us with an eminently practical guide to the cultural map, or maps, we inhabit and within which we act" (p. 41). Grierson notes that making sense is never the result of passive reflection. An individual's common sense is comprised of theories that have been borrowed and constructed from experience.

These are open to modification and change. Common sense is inherently grounded in our own practice and at the same time undergirds practice.

It's Okay Not to Be Perfect

Candice recalls that Kay does a lot of consulting with colleagues *and* with the children. "Like a book isn't going well, a read-aloud let's say. She'll ask the kids, 'What do you think about this? Let's talk about it.' She was always asking me and other student teachers." Kay does not hide her struggles from student teachers or from the children. "She was at the board and something was going wrong and she would be like, 'Candice, where do you think we should go from here?'... her entire classroom is set up with the whole theory of cooperative learning." She models collaboration and consultation for the children and student teachers. And she makes them feel that it is okay not to be perfect.

Brenda points out, "She really got it through to me that it was okay to experiment with my teaching style. It took me the first half of the semester. . . . But she really assured me that it was okay." Candice remembers a cursive handwriting lesson that was "pure chaos. The kids just weren't following, and they were talking and struggling with the letters, and I had problems managing them." Afterwards, when Candice was feeling like a failure, Kay snapped her out of it. "Okay, that was chaos. What can we do differently?" Candice was taken with how untroubled Kay was by the disaster. She was matter-of-fact: A problem had been identified, and they needed to figure out how to solve it.

Kay works with the children in the same way. As she moves throughout the room during group work time, she will get down to eye level and say to a group of children who are not working, "So if we're having a problem, what could we do about it? Can somebody think of one thing you could try?" or "Maybe you should try something else."

Kay's experimental attitude toward teaching is indicative of how she has attempted to make sense of things, or developed and tested practical theory. It is a strong thread throughout her career, one identified during her first semester of student teaching, and the means by which she develops new strategies for working with children. In Elliott's (1976–77) opinion, "If teachers are not modifying their teaching behavior over time, one has good grounds for assuming that they are not testing and developing theory" (p. 8). It is, perhaps, her ability to study events and frame them as problems to be solved, her "practical theorizing," that most enables Kay to deal with issues of classroom management and control, another barrier to deliberative, reflective teaching.

GETTING PAST THE CONTROL BARRIER

In Chapter 1, I introduced the bleak prospect that despite her motivation to be a caring teacher, Kay is at risk of becoming more concerned about control than about issues of teaching and learning. Authoritative and controlling practices that seem to work in the moment are likely to replace reflective, deliberative practice and experimentation (Arnstine, 1990). Britzman (1986) argues that the student teacher's image of schools and schooling along with the immediate demands of school, classroom, and students frame the way they will respond to student teaching and how they will develop as teachers. Classroom control is such a pervasive need that it is likely to replace learning. Britzman postulates that as student teachers focus on control, they repress their own desire to explore and be open. While experience is always instructive, it may perpetuate things as they are, rather than challenging the existing power arrangements. In Britzman's view, examining biography, particularly one's institutional biography, helps develop a critical stance toward school dynamics.

It is the meanings associated with experience that have been most powerful in shaping who we are. These past experiences are continuously being reconstructed in light of the present. Sometimes it is difficult, if not impossible, for an individual to understand the patterns of thinking and acting that have developed through personal experience, but noticing them is a key step.

Rather than asking student teachers to reflect on their institutional biography and cultural myths, it would seem more sensible to ask them to reflect on their own theories of development, teaching, and learning, and how these have emerged from past experience. They can then compare these to both educational and psychological theories and test and strengthen them in the classroom, utilizing theories (including their own) in an experimental way. The social and political ramifications of particular forms of knowledge, school structures, mechanisms of control, and individual choice are understood as givens from the beginning because students have examined their own social construction of knowledge. To stimulate such thinking, Kay and other students in the preservice program are asked to complete a study of their school site, examining it along a series of social and political dimensions.

Being a Student of School Culture

Kay recalls that interviewing teachers, parents, and school administrators along with a team of student teachers helped her to realize the complexity of the school. "When I first came here I thought, 'Wow, this school really runs great! Everything you know, is so beautiful!' And you realize, not *that* beautiful!" Being challenged to become an activist for change made a lasting impression as well. "Obviously there wouldn't be a reason to say anything [through the school study] if there wasn't going to be a political agenda there." When she entered the program as a new college graduate, Kay felt that she was unprepared for the politics in any organization, much less the school. Learning to listen to the context and learn from it helped, but it did not completely prepare her for the reality she experienced once she became a teacher at the school, "Like . . . how fast gossips zips through this place and how much it's cliquey, there's a lot of cliques. . . . I became very friendly with people here and they became friends of mine. . . . I wasn't prepared for how much my personal life might affect my professional life. . . . I don't know how you can prepare somebody for that."

Yet teaching and teacher education, as human endeavors, are "unavoidably political enterprises" (Cochran-Smith, 2000, p. 165). And schools, as centers of human activity, will be political. Teachers' rooms and school corridors are notoriously centers of gossip about children and their families. They are places where other teachers are critiqued and included or excluded from the underlying power structure.

Kay is not perceived as someone who gave in to the cliques and the gossip that characterized her school. This is illustrated in an episode involving an unsuccessful student teacher, Jed. While Candice was interning with her, Kay was assigned an additional student teacher from another college. The student was problematic in a number of ways. Jed seemed to have difficulty deciding what was appropriate for children and what was not. After I had first met him during a supervisory visit to Candice, Kay pulled me aside and said that he was in a very different place from Candice in terms of experience and skill, but that she hoped she would be able to move him along. She was, typically, very matter of fact and professional. She identifies the problem, frames it as a puzzle to figure out, studies it, and experiments with solutions.

Candice's reaction was intense and personal. Her journal is full of comments about Jed and her frustration with him. "He annoyed the hell out of me," she recalled years later.

> My whole journal is about this . . . sexist pig! Kay only made one or two comments about him, and they were always very noncommittal, and it wasn't until I went out to dinner with her and I was no longer in her classroom that she said to me, "I could not stand Jed!" Like she always kept that very professional level.

Despite her various interventions, Jed does not respond as Kay hopes he will. She considers asking the college to remove him from her room and decides, instead, to give him very specific and limited tasks. Although there is a great deal of comment from other teachers who notice him with children in the hallways or on the playground, Kay refrains from gossip. In contrast, Candice's cooperating teacher the following semester constantly complains about another student teacher and solicits her opinion of him. "So I think that [Kay's] sense of professionalism, hey it makes her a leader. I think that one reason there isn't a lot of gossip in the group of people she hangs out with [is] because she just doesn't tolerate it." Candice recalls that instead of gossip, she gave curriculum tips or suggestions about good resources. The conversations were friendly, comfortable, and professional.

Getting a Grip

Kay wants to be a part of the school culture without necessarily buying into the negative dynamics. At the same time, she has to find her own footing with classroom discipline. As an intern, the structure and discipline began with Susan and transferred to her. As the teacher, she had to make her own way. The issue of discipline is one that all beginning teachers face and that most often traps them in negative patterns of reinforcing misbehavior. In her second year of teaching, Kay has a particularly challenging fourth-grade class. In describing one episode, Khristine writes in her journal:

> Kay's had a terribly rough 2 days. She was constantly on the verge of losing her temper all day and in fact did lose it once. The children are wild and completely incapable of handling responsibility right now. Kay is frustrated because she enjoys teaching with a relatively open style, but the children just goof around. Even when they have plenty to do, like a math packet or project research, many children wander around. I think what exacerbates the situation is that a few children physically taunt and harm each other. Lack of productivity is one thing—causing physical harm is another.

The class continues to challenge Kay, and Khristine separates herself from the situation, trying to critique, but often criticizing Kay for trying to get the children's attention by forcing her voice above theirs. One day, admitting that she is exhausted and doesn't have the energy to yell, Kay sits and waits for children to get quiet. She treats their reaction as an experiment and wonders if it will work again. She notices that another teacher uses a hand signal to get the children's attention and decides they should try it, too. Khristine continues to try to analyze the situation in her own way:

> I recognize Kay's struggle and wonder what she could have done differently to prevent the negative group dynamic. . . . I think about this class in terms of next year and wonder what I would do—I take comfort in the idea that the class dynamic would never get this bad because I would have taken pains to be firm and structured from the beginning. But then I wonder whether or not Kay could have changed the way things worked out. Could a teacher still have this situation if she does everything "right"?

Khristine is still buying into the cultural myth that it all depends on the teacher and blames Kay for failing to prevent the situation from happening. Meanwhile, Kay continues to experiment. She sets up a behavior modification system to deal with the problems, rewarding tables with points for appropriate behavior—a system she will return to when she faces another challenging class during her fourth year as a teacher. Khristine, who maintains a critical stance throughout the semester, views Kay's struggle with discipline differently once she has her own classroom. She reflects on the experience 3 years later. "I now understand more than I did when I stood there watching it." She, too, has grown from the experience.

> What stands out from that year was she had a really tough group of kids. And I remember her saying that. I had a rough group this year, so her whole thing that she was saying then really made sense this year. I remember she would say, "This is, this part is going so much slower than I would expect it to, and what do I need to figure out to get these guys to come around?" She had a difficult bunch of kids in that room that year.

Khristine recalls that Kay was constantly trying to figure out how to deal with the group and with individual children. One child was particularly "nasty," Khristine thought, and when she complained, Kay pointed out that the girl had made enormous progress during the year. "And there were a few kids who stood out in that way, so she would talk about the steps she took to bring them along to where they were at the point that I met them."

In her first semester of student teaching, Kay worried for fear that Janet would actually give up on a child and was relieved to know that she didn't. Kay's constant struggle to find ways to help children and refusal to give up is a noticeable characteristic that connects to her own experiences with justice and injustice as a student. Khristine recalls:

> I know that there were some children who were particularly troubling her. She was worried about them. A little boy, his mom was out on the street. Kay would meet with the mom on the street because she was a, I guess, a prostitute or something. Another one, we went to camp that year, and one of the children couldn't go and she really worked with the dad. We thought it might be cultural, it wasn't financial, he was just afraid and she was saying how nice that would have been. That child in particular needed to go to camp, he needed that experience and he wasn't going to have it.

Like most beginning teachers, Kay does not get it all right in a year. But, perhaps unlike many, she does not blame herself for systemic failures and sees management issues as integrally related to curriculum and context. And she no longer buys into the cultural myth that it all depends on the teacher that she, like Khristine, accepted as a student teacher. And she approaches control issues with the experimental mindset that has allowed her to grow in managing the classroom over time.

In glimpses of Kay in action during her third year of teaching, we notice that she acknowledges feelings when children become frustrated with a handwriting lesson: "Cursive is hard for some people." She organizes so there will not be discipline issues by setting up procedures for storage and use of materials, reminding Jessie to "take away anything the children aren't using so they won't be distracted" when she is trying to get their attention. She leads children to analyze their own behavior through questioning: "Can we all talk at once?" She reminds them of the rules and gives them alternatives: "If you don't want to stay here and listen, I want you to go back to your desk." She elicits the behavior she desires rather than rewarding undesirable behavior: "When you're ready, sit quietly in your seat. That is how I will know you are ready. Table six is ready." And she does not hesitate to call a halt and restate a rule if things seem out of control: "*Stop!* Nobody is allowed to touch anyone else during a meeting." And when her best efforts do not create the desired overall classroom order, she reinstitutes the table point system she developed with her previous class in order to motivate the children to keep the noise level down and follow directions. Consistent with her interest in teaching children how to work collaboratively, the points go to the group rather than to individual children.

Linking Curriculum and Control

Kay constantly studies the children and experiments with ways to deal with classroom control issues. But it is primarily through getting the children involved in the curriculum that Kay attempts to deal with discipline. When we talk together just after she had completed her fifth year of teaching, Kay does not separate issues of management from curricular questions. She reflects on how she makes curriculum decisions:

> Sometimes the choices I make are based on how many kids it can affect. I mean, if it's going to help one kid, but yet not help anybody else, I might just not be able to do it. Whereas if whatever it is can help a few kids, its more likely I would do it. That's one factor. A lot of it, though, saying that, then I sort of go the other way, too. A lot of it just depends on the child. A lot of it is done based on what that child needs then. Like I might say one year, "This is how I'm dealing with my academically bottom kids," whereas another year it's different, depending on what their personalities are. It's hard to say what really decides my curriculum—unfortunately, time is a huge factor.

She tries to balance the needs of individuals and groups:

> Which definitely comes into play with the discipline problems. You know, I know that if I do this with this child, it might help that one child, but sometimes it's just not fair to the 27 other kids for me to take the time to do that. If it's a discipline thing, it just might have to wait.

The fact that Kay always connects management issues with the curriculum is probably one of the reasons that control issues never dominate her. When Kay makes a decision about the curriculum, she thinks of the larger picture:

> Is it worth all that I'm going to put into it or that the child's going to put into it in order to do it; is making them write something beautifully, is that going to give them the self confidence that they can do it, or is it going to torment them and make it not worth it?

I asked her what happens if things aren't working, despite her careful planning. Her immediate response is, "It depends how it's not working!" She laughs.

> If it's not working because all of a sudden there is bedlam in here, you know . . . if it's not working because they're not getting it, you know, like we're doing some math lesson and they're just, the majority is just going, "I can't do this! I can't do . . . ," then in the middle of the lesson I probably will call it to a halt, call them all back in, and decide if we need to wait to go on to it till the next day until I can figure it out again or, you know, pull it back or whatever. But I've definitely done that in the middle of lessons that aren't working. Just to say . . . "hold on."

She continues, "And I've also gotten to the point where I ask my kids, like, 'What aren't you getting?' like 'Where did you start losing it?' you know, that kind of thing. I've started doing that more and more than I had before." She also talks with other teachers about what they've tried.

Kay's tendency to frame challenges as problems that can be addressed and to understand herself as a student of teaching is an enduring ingredient of her makeup as a teacher. Now in her tenth year as a teacher, she still reflects on the teacher she would like to be:

> Well, it would be somebody who is . . . able to hit each kid's strength and make them expand on their strength and make them feel really good about themselves because of it and also build up their deficit so that it doesn't go by the wayside—which I think, unfortunately, too many times [it] does. The other thing is I would have the kids really feel comfortable about interacting with each other, asking each other for help, but giving each other help in suggestions, not just "That's the answer" kind of help but "What do you think of this?" kind of help. [Comfortable] with them and with me, having the same kind of conversations, "What do you think of this?" You know, having them to be comfortable to come to me all the time and vice versa, my feeling comfortable enough to say to them, "What do you think abut that?—Do you think that would work that way?" and have a discussion about it versus their just taking my word for it because I'm the teacher.

She reflects on this ideal:

> I don't know if I emphasized that as much when I first started teaching, the kind of conversation kids would have. I knew I always wanted them to work together, but the ways they are doing it has changed over the years. I've worked hard so that they don't get defensive whenever a suggestion is made, that they feel free to

make suggestions to others, or try to, working to that ideal. I think I've focused more on that give-and-take amongst the kids in my later years. In the beginning it's really all about them just working together and getting their stuff out and creating a product they all felt good about together, but it wasn't as much that discussions of like, "Hey, you can use this." Real conversation over what the process was versus just doing it together. I don't think I realized that when I first started grouping, that working in a group has to take that direction, it's not just, "Okay, she does one part, she does another part, he does another part, and they can get up and share it together."

Her program equipped her to work with both children and adults in cooperative groups. It may be the latter—working with adults—that kept Kay actively reflecting on her own practice.

MAKING REFLECTION COMPATIBLE WITH SCHOOL LIFE

The goals of reflective teacher preparation are incompatible with those of most schools, particularly complex urban schools. Life in the classroom is fast-paced, and schools are under constant pressure to raise achievement scores. We have already seen how tests place pressure on Kay to adjust the curriculum. But dealing with the pressure has been eased by a school environment that encourages collaboration and by Kay's own inclination to work with other teachers.

Candice notices that on the first day of school Kay goes to both first-year teachers, who were also teaching second grade. "She checked on both of them to make sure they were okay. Asked them if they have slept, if they have eaten. Said you better eat, you know, like when they came in at lunch and they were all jittery." She was not only interested in them personally; she also asked them about the classroom, "questions like, 'How do you know this?' and then she said 'How long were they on the rug?' " when things broke down. She said, "You need to get them up and down and you need to do this and this. It was like logical, and the way that she said it was real friendly." The result was that teachers did not feel threatened. In fact, Kay asked them for information, too. Brenda describes her as being "very good at creating a family of colleagues."

A family of colleagues is critical to Kay's reflection on her own practice. Getting new teachers together keeps her thinking about her teaching. In one of our coffee meetings during Kay's sixth year as a teacher, we talk about the importance of collaboration in keeping the reflective process alive. She talks about the four colleagues on her grade level that she meets with regularly, the group Brenda has described. "Well, four of us plan together a lot. . . . We'll get together, it was like two or three times a week in the beginning of the year—now it's once a week—and brainstorm all together." It is the first year for two of the teachers and the first year teaching third grade for another. As they all talk about what they are doing in their own classrooms, they look to Kay. "They would say, 'Well, why do you do this?' or 'How would I do this?' and it made me think about it a lot. I probably did a lot more reflecting on my teaching this year than any other year because they asked the questions." Kay laughs. "So I had to think up the answers, you know!"

The group engages in group curriculum planning. Building on curriculum design strategies she learned as a preservice student, Kay leads them in making a web. But her work in thinking through the curriculum also continues apart from the group:

> So a lot of it was that group kind of planning, but, for myself, I think I always start a curriculum and sort of just write down everything I think I'm going—all my ideas of what I can do, then go through the mapping out a little bit and then get down to the individual lesson.

Kay thinks collaborative planning has made a difference in her teaching. When something doesn't work, she can ask other people if they've tried it and how it went.

> Yeah, and what usually happens is like two of us have gotten it done and been like, "Oh my god!" you know, *"Don't* do it!"— Either that or they'll say, you know, "Do it with half the class" or "Do it with . . . "—you know, whatever. So that's actually good the way it happens that we give each other clues along the way. . . . If someone else has done it, I will definitely talk to them about it and see. If not, I sit and think, and think about it and say, "Did this not work because this lesson is not worth doing and they're just not going to get it?" or "Did it not work because we did it in smaller groups, do we need to do it in two lessons, do we need to do it?" Those are probably the first questions I ask. "Was it too much at once? Was it something worth doing? What are they going to get out of all this at the end of it?"—that kind of stuff, and then think through, like, "How could I have explained it better?" or whatever.

For Kay, the process is more important than products at the end. Starting with how a curriculum will end is too restrictive. If the focus is only on predetermined objectives, there is little room for imagination or for children to discover new, perhaps more important, ends. An appropriate process will lead to creative, imaginative, and important outcomes. For Kay, it is just as important to think about a process and possible ends. "I've found, no matter what I start with, often it will go another way or a lot longer. . . . Other ideas come up, you know, the kids come up with ideas, or another teacher—one thing just leads into something else."

Thinking about how to make her curriculum inclusive, so that it reflects her children, has kept Kay thinking about her work. Her curriculum *is* inclusive. She uses a variety of multicultural stories, and the classroom library is full of books about many cultures. For example, when they are studying immigration, Kay reads a book about a girl's Russian ancestors to her third-grade class. She picks up on the grandfather character who tells tall tales. "Why would the grandfather exaggerate like that?" she asks. Children offer several ideas. Manuel thinks he might have wanted to impress her. Evan suggests, "Maybe he didn't want to make her sad because the way it was [was] really sad." Ariel supposes that it was what the grandfather wished.

Kay's response to these ideas is animated—"Wow . . . great!" She uses the children's ideas to initiate a discussion of idioms. "We're going to do something about these exaggerated stories." They talk about the idiom "It's raining cats and dogs." Each table gets one idiom about immigrating to the United States, with the directions that they are to talk about it and to be prepared to explain what it really means.

Kay sees the program's emphasis on cultural diversity as critical in helping her to deal with the reality of urban schools. "I definitely read the articles on it, when I had to choose. That was something I was really interested in at the time and still am. So I did feel like I did get a lot of background." Kay does not want to be in a school like the one she attended, which was "a 90% homogeneous school, so working here and articles I read" prepared her "certainly to think about it. And I've learned stuff along the way just dealing with parents—a lot comes up, you know, and the kids, but I think I was definitely predisposed, prepared to consider that when I was coming into the classroom." She recalls how her child study opened her eyes to her own tendency to make negative judgments about a child's home environment. She had described her child as being a product of a one-parent family, and in the preservice core, we emphasized that one must not pass judgment. "I'll never forget Lin [one of the program directors] saying, 'Don't make assumptions!'"

Being involved in collaborative curriculum planning has been one way in which Kay has dealt with the pressure of an urban school and the highly political climate of the PDS. But her location in the PDS is also a protection from the grim realities of many urban school environments. The PDS does not have the complexity of many urban schools. Although it began as a school that had been all but abandoned by middle-class families, it has since become a highly desirable school and has had to struggle to keep a diverse population of students as the surrounding neighborhood has become more and more upscale. Kay thinks about this, remembering her experiences in Ithaca, when she first became interested in working in urban schools. She confesses to feeling guilty about it and wonders if things have been too comfortable for her.

> You know, I love being able to tell people I teach in New York City! And I feel proud of that fact—the fact is I feel proud that I have 30 kids in a class with all these different backgrounds and I'm dealing with it, but there is still that nudge that feels like I can do more. But then part of me is like, especially those first years of teaching was like, "Don't do it your first couple of years! Wait and see what you're doing." That's part of the reason why I'm now looking for other avenues to go.

The other avenues turn out to be serving as a member of the clinical faculty at TC and eventually, in her ninth year, moving to a school location nearer family. When a job offer came she "got excited about the job" because it was in "one of the few school districts on Long Island that is somewhat diverse in ethnicity and economically." Having spent a year working in a reading support program during her last year in New York City, Kay recalls that she "wanted to go back into the classroom but somewhere new. Bottom line, I needed some big changes to get me excited about teaching again." She had not enjoyed her role outside the classroom.

Even though her present school is economically and culturally diverse, Kay confesses that while it might be seen as "the typical move to the suburbs," it has stretched her:

> In some ways my teaching has required even more effort on my part because I do not have people around me that all teach as I do, though there are some, and I have to constantly reexamine my teaching for what I believe as well as how it will come across to the parents and administration.

After 9 years in a complex, urban school, Kay is finding that her new suburban–urban school also offers her many opportunities to keep learning.

CONCLUSION

A group of factors seem to be obstacles to attracting and retaining academically able teachers in the profession—barriers to Kay's otherwise promising future as a deliberative teacher. The word *barriers* evokes many images, including the image of an obstacle course or a track-and-field event. We imagine Kay getting ready for a cross-country championship in which runners face appalling conditions to win what is often called the most difficult of track-and-field competitions. Kay lines up, she is off—we see her running and cheer her along as she meets one obstacle after another with mental discipline and physical grit. But the metaphor does not work. Kay as runner is not an adequate image because the barriers described in the literature are not a series of conditions to be run through, like mud and sand, but a set of realities that present themselves simultaneously and continuously. In reality, Kay has not passed the barriers—she has learned to deal with them as they present and re-present themselves. Her self-reflective approach to teaching and inclination to experiment are part of a process that has served her well. Collaboration and curriculum planning have been integral to her success, too. And she has had levels of support that not many teachers can claim by virtue of her location in a PDS.

The one negative prospect that we can say she has actually overcome and left behind is that of dropping out within her first 5 years of teaching. We can assume that she circumvented this possibility because the other barriers had been overcome. But there may be more to it. We will reflect on this in the chapter to follow as we contrast her career trajectory with that of two other women who graduated from the preservice program without the benefit of being part of the PDS.

ಐ 8 ಐ

Learning to Teach:
A Continuous Reconstruction

> I definitely remember leadership being talked about a lot in
> the program, like being an activist, you know, taking your
> stand. . . . I think that a lot of those ideas that were about,
> "Get up and do something about it"—that push definitely
> got me going, like joining school-based management here. I
> think a lot of that talk got me to start doing things. The pro-
> fessional development school, recently, is pushing me more
> to do stuff than it did in the very beginning.
> —Kay, May 1996

TEACHING IS a profession that suits Kay. She has found it more satisfying
than frustrating. Teaching allows her to have fun, to fulfill her impulse
toward social justice, and to continue learning, experimenting, and growing as a person in ways that are consistent with her beliefs about life. These
beliefs, while tempered by her preservice program and her experience in
schools, have remained remarkably stable. But they have grown beyond
the immature understanding of teaching, schools, and learning that
marked Kay's entry into teaching. Her personal knowledge has been and
continues to be reconstructed. Looking at her career allows us to speculate
with her about what has kept her in teaching, but it cannot answer the
question for us. Although she points to various frustrations and satisfac-
tions with her work, there is probably no one factor that has kept her in
teaching. Even if there were a definitive answer to why she has stayed,
it would be unlikely to be the answer for all academically able teachers.

One thing does seem clear, however. Kay has had more than the
usual amount of support for entry into the profession and as a beginning
teacher. Therefore, before we draw conclusions about what her career
path might teach us, we will consider her career in relation to two other
academically able women who also completed the TC preservice program
more than a decade ago. Angela has been in and out of teaching over the

years. Luisa has stayed in the classroom. We look at brief profiles of these two women along with Kay, asking what their experiences can tell us about how to prepare and support deliberative teachers.

ANGELA—IN AND OUT OF THE CLASSROOM

Angela wanted to teach because "I thought it would be creative. I thought it would be fun, nurturing." She has been in and out of teaching since graduating from the preservice program in the early 1990s. Angela took a job at a boarding school in Connecticut, where she taught for 2 years before taking a 4-year hiatus from education to go to law school. She returned to teaching after a year of practicing law because she missed the children. "Even when I went to law school, I got involved with a middle school and coached soccer. They said, 'Why don't you just go back to teaching? Because that's what you seem to like to do.' " Since then she has held a variety of teaching jobs in public and private schools in New York City and in nearby Connecticut suburbs. Although she never stayed in one school for more than 2 years, she spent about 6½ years in classroom teaching. But after searching for the right spot, Angela became fed up with the bureaucracy of schools. "So I found a way to do what I love but not be tied into this bureaucracy that I think is ridiculous." She decided to "go private" and established a tutoring service for learning-disabled students.

> I love it because I get to help kids one-on-one. I get to do a lot of assessment. I am not tied into, um,—like a lot of time kids don't get services because of money issues, politics. So I don't have that. I can do whatever I want. When I want to take vacation, I just go. When I don't want to, I stay. And, um, I also get to study a lot more; again, about the latest research being done with learning, which is fascinating.

The decision to leave classroom teaching was neither straightforward nor uncomplicated. Angela more or less fell into her interest in working intensively with children who have special learning needs. Initially, she was frustrated with the way such children were dealt with by the school system and began taking some courses to equip herself to help them in the regular classroom. She discovered that there was a demand for out-of-school support for children with special learning needs when she began doing some tutoring on the side. The demand for her service pointed to what may become a new and successful career path for Angela. In the meantime, she is off for an extended trip to the Australian outback.

In following Kay's career trajectory, we have seen the place of personal knowledge in her forming of self as a teacher. Angela's trajectory is also consistent with her personal knowledge, and her beliefs about education are encapsulated in early memories. Angela recalls being in preschool:

> I have this one memory of—it's a bad memory—we were all in this music class. And the teacher asked everyone to clap to the music. So everyone did their own like thing in the way they clapped to the music. And I clapped and I snapped my fingers, you know, like one after the other. And she stopped and she said . . .

Angela's voice gets syrupy sweet as she imitates the music teacher:

> "That's really good, Angela. Can you do that for everyone?" And I cried and I got really scared. And I never wanted to go back to school. . . . I felt put on the spot. I was personally a really sensitive child. So, like, you just couldn't single me out like that. It made me feel really self-conscious. And I knew she loved me and I loved the school, too, but it's just that one incident just scared me.

Angela's positive recollection is less specific but nevertheless important in helping us understand her passion for learning.

> I remember . . . that we used to always have this fair and they used to have *The Red Balloon*, the French movie. And I thought it was so great to see Paris and *The Red Balloon*. . . . I don't even remember what it was really about. It was this boy and the red balloon. Maybe to me it was just so enchanting.

In reflecting on her own experiences, Angela wants teachers to be sensitive to the uniqueness of each child, to see what is special about each. And teachers should not make assumptions about children. "There are kids who are very sensitive." These children should be "treated with kid gloves." How children feel about school is crucial to Angela. School should be a place where they want to be and where they feel safe.

At the outset of the preservice program, Angela talked about wanting to teach her students "to be passionate about life, to embrace everything around," perhaps to be touched as she was touched by *The Red Balloon* and images of Paris. She wanted "to make a difference . . . change the world somehow and improve society." Angela's motivation to teach was grounded in memories of teachers who were "nurturing role models" and "mother figures." These were people who seemed to understand her well and made school a safe place where she could develop as a person—they changed her world and made a difference in what she describes as a difficult childhood. As she began her preparation, Angela hoped to provide a similar, nurturing environment for students. Teachers were important models for her, and she wanted to be a good model. Throughout her two semesters of core and student teaching, she was constantly wondering whether she was being "the best teacher" for the children and whether she could really be a model for students from backgrounds dramatically different from her own.

As an adult, returning to school, Angela was looking for school to be a safe haven where passion and imagination were engaged. She wanted school to be a place where she belonged, where students belonged, and by this she meant that she and they were known, heard, and understood. Belonging is a central theme in Angela's papers, student-teaching journals, and conversations. And there were moments of great success when school "fit"—for example, when she taught an innovative, interdisciplinary curriculum that was hands-on, involving children in community service to clean up Long Island Sound. It was publicized in the local media.

> We were making a difference. The most important thing was kids loved coming to school and they learned all that stuff—easily— you know, including reading and math and all that *and* they have made a permanent difference in our community and they made the world a better place . . . that's what I believe teaching should be.

But there is a sense in which Angela never really belonged in school as the teacher. She was constantly frustrated by the institution of schooling. She was restless. As a teacher, she felt that she was not heard or acknowledged and was not trusted, respected, or appropriately compensated as a competent professional. These feelings were in part due to what she saw as the bureaucratic structure of schools.

> I can't stand the fact that the Board of Ed is not made up of teachers. It's businesspeople who don't know anything about children, and yet they are making decisions that are very important. I think it's absolutely ridiculous the way it's run. I think the whole thing should be knocked down and re-redone.

Despite the emphasis on collaboration in the program, Angela did not seem to find many opportunities to collaborate with teacher colleagues or be part of a school as a learning community. She remembers the experience of collaborative planning with a third-grade teacher as "warm and friendly," one in which "we worked through things to get to a common thought. We shared ideas. We were not in competition. We truly respected each other." But this was an exceptional experience. For the most part, Angela saw herself as apart from other teachers. As a student in the preservice program, she often distanced herself from other students as she expressed frustration with them for not taking things as seriously as she does. As a teacher, she was frustrated when colleagues became part of an oppressive system either by buying into policies or failing to stand up for themselves.

Angela sees teaching as an intellectual activity and believes teachers should be scholars. "Teachers should be held to very high expectations and should be paid a lot more money because we should be thought of in that way." Law school appealed to her because it fed her intellectually and demanded rigor. She believes that teaching is no less rigorous and demanding, but that too often teachers are working from superficial knowledge. She uses mathematics, one of her own interests, as an example:

> I mean, I see so many teachers who know nothing about the history of mathematics and numbers, when it comes to math. They just kind of learn how to do addition and subtraction and they teach it. That's not teaching people to be brilliant thinkers, that's just teaching math. And kids get bored, especially smart kids.

In a sense, Angela is the "smart kid who gets bored" with teaching. She finds the intellectual work of curriculum design and the crafting of learning episodes to be the most exciting and challenging aspects of teaching. For Angela, reflective activities and curriculum development are the most important parts of the program core. "Self-reflection" she explains, "leads to great growth" and offers the potential to help teachers "become good teachers instead of being a body in a classroom, reading a textbook, and giving questions." But too much of teaching does not honor Angela's interest in curriculum development or self-reflection. And too many headmasters and principals "will not risk their jobs for the benefit of children . . . even if what's going on in the school is not good for children."

Without the opportunity to engage deeply in intellectual activity, Angela does not feel at home in the classroom. "And I've put my job on the line so many times to stand up for what I believe is right for children."

In short, school has not been the welcoming, safe place Angela remembers from childhood, and, as an adult, it does not offer her enough intellectual stimulation to hold her.

When asked what would have to change to keep her in the classroom, Angela talks about economic rewards, freedom, and creativity:

> The pay is ridiculous. . . . You must do this. You must call in. . . . You must punch in in the morning. . . . What I didn't get was the ability to be creative. There's too many standardized curriculums and we don't get to write our own curriculum. Creativity and intelligence is not valued and brilliance is not rewarded.

Angela has stayed with teaching, if not with schools, because, "I just think it's the most important job on this planet. Yeah. And I think I'm very good at it."

LUISA—FINDING THE RIGHT SCHOOL

Luisa has been teaching for 8 years, 7 at a public alternative school in upper Manhattan. Her desire to teach is rooted in education as a family value. "I want to teach [my students] how to love themselves and learn to appreciate all the beauty that life has to offer," she wrote as an entering student in the preservice program. Like Angela and Kay, she was also motivated by a strong sense of social justice. For Luisa, however, this has to do with her identity as Hispanic. "I've just been learning about myself lately, but I think I've come to the realization that I want to help *my* people," she wrote during her second semester of student teaching. These two themes—love of learning and cultural identity—persist in her career.

To become the teacher she hoped to be, Luisa had to overcome not only the barriers facing prospective teachers such as Kay and Angela but also another barrier facing academically able Hispanic and African Americans. A disproportionately small number of minority students, particularly Hispanic youth, enroll in postsecondary education as compared to Whites. Furthermore, minorities drop out at a higher rate than other teachers do (Bolin, 1994).

Luisa began to work as a full-time secretary for the New Teacher Recruitment and Retention Project, funded by the Pew Charitable Trusts, during her first few weeks of the program. As director of the project, I began to involve her in the life of the project, and she became active in helping to develop a support system for minority and nontraditional students in teacher-preparation programs across the college and to visit college campuses to recruit minority students into teaching. Working full time meant that she took longer to complete her program than either Kay or Angela. But, as the sole caretaker for a younger brother, it was an economic necessity.

Like Angela, Luisa experienced school as a safe place and saw teachers as role models and nurturing figures. It was just after Luisa's fifth birthday that she moved to the United States and entered "an unknown world, filled with many strangers [who] all tried to talk to me and make me feel welcome, but I didn't understand a word!" Her kindergarten experience "marked a new beginning. That year changed my life forever. At the end of that year I could speak English, I learned basic scholastic skills, I learned how to share, make friends, and play games." In fact, Luisa's first memory of school is "being in kindergarten, crying all the time because I didn't understand what was happening." She describes it as hard, but "once I understood what was happening, I just loved being there. I always remember having fun. I remember being the good kid— you sit quiet and you do your work, listen and ask questions." It is not surprising that she believed that, for her, the role of teacher included being a model for minority students. In fact, during her first semester of student teaching, she identified a newly immigrated student for her child study. "I try to make a special effort to make her feel as welcome and comfortable in her new surroundings as possible." During her second semester, Luisa broadened her idea of being a role model when she was placed in an affluent school. She realized that her fourth-graders needed the experience of working with a competent, intelligent minority teacher as much as did the girl she chose to follow in her child study.

Luisa's early positive recollection is about moving to another school for first grade. "The first day I went to this school, I met a friend. Like the girl that the teacher says, 'Can you sit next to her and she'll help you?' And I met a friend, you know, and she was with me all my life. She's now my best friend." Luisa saw this experience finding expression in her own teaching:

> I can see when the kids are having problems with their close friends and how important it is for them to be able to talk it out and share their feelings and to be able to communicate. Sometimes it's just allowing, creating that space for them to talk, one to one, so they have the chance to do that.

Luisa recalls making other friends—African American, Haitian American, Irish, Italian, Hispanic. She recalls other instances involving friendship that are not so happy. One powerful memory is going home after school with an Italian friend to study. The girl's father made her leave because "he says he doesn't allow Black people in his house," and Luisa was told never to come back. She remembers, too, confessing that she liked an Irish boy to a girlfriend who said that she didn't know Black people could like White people.

Luisa had not thought of herself as being different from other children. Race and culture were never talked about in school. These experiences challenged Luisa to seek a culturally, racially diverse school setting and create a classroom environment that consciously, visibly honored diversity—a place where everybody belongs. Luisa describes her current school as a place "where there is diversity, and it's valued, and it's talked about. . . . We talk about stereotypes, we talk about gender roles, we talk about all this stuff." She says of her students, "I know I'm forming a whole little person, their minds are more open to what, you know, society is really like."

Luisa recalls that the TC program played an important role in her development as a teacher, though it in no way fully prepared her. She sees the curriculum development, school study, and observation as the critical pieces the program contributed to her growth "and an ability to look at my work and think about it." In fact, observation and reflection are still cornerstones of Luisa's teaching, which she describes as "learning how to see." But the preservice program was also significant because "It was my first time *ever* having a teacher of color. *Ever.*"

As Luisa neared completion of the preservice program, she was eager to work in a challenging urban school and accepted a job at a public school in the Bronx. It was "sink or swim," she recalls, and "I was really, really scared—terrified. I didn't feel prepared." She experienced alienation from colleagues who were not eager to question existing school arrangements, as Luisa's preservice program had challenged and equipped her to do. Dealing with alienation was a hard reality. Luisa recalls that "once I got started I began to feel that I *was* prepared and I had something to offer." But this in itself presented problems:

> I wanted to go in and share ideas. Everyone was pretty much to themselves. I felt I knew a lot more than most of the people there. The administration told everyone what to do and they went along. It bugged me. I wanted to have critical discussions [see Bolin, 1994].

Furthermore, Luisa, whose English is impeccable, was confronted with another stereotype, this time coming from Hispanic colleagues. "There was this feeling: If you're Hispanic, you should associate only with Hispanics." Her speech isolated her from Hispanic colleagues, who seemed to think she should be speaking with an accent and resented the fact that she associated with everyone. When she went to other teachers for mentoring, Hispanic colleagues made her feel as if "you're not one of us. You're one of them." Luisa did not want to choose sides. She recognized discontinuity between the school's espoused goal of empowering its largely Hispanic population and school rules and structures that told everyone what to do, what to teach, what to learn, what to think. "If you're going to teach them [students] to think you have to ask them, 'What do you think about this?' . . . I want them to question. I want them to be leaders." Luisa wanted her colleagues to question and think, too.

By spring, Luisa was more and more worn down by the school environment. She needed a school culture that would say yes to her abilities and skills, rather than one that was constantly saying no. Luisa had stayed in touch with faculty and colleagues in the preservice program during that difficult year. She was encouraged to find a place where she could work with an urban population, but where she also had some support. She found such a place through a friend. It was a school that was just a year old, a school that was formed through the efforts of parents who wanted a viable, progressive, diverse public school. The school was in sharp contrast to the rigid, restrictive environment in which she had spent her first year.

Luisa has been at this school ever since. She recalls how teachers who are both intelligent and interesting mentored her. "It pushed me to widen myself as a person, you know. I think when you just first start teaching you get so sucked into the room you forget to develop as a person. I'll never forget them, they're amazing." The school environment supports the kind of reflection she valued in the preservice program and longed for in her first year. "As a staff, we're always reading a lot of professional literature, we're always going to different conferences and being exposed to different ideas." And teachers talk about their own experiences in school—"what pieces of that were helpful and what pieces of that weren't."

She values and still uses the observational skills she learned through studying a child and the school as a preservice student. She sees herself as a continuous learner, and she is constantly studying, observing children, and inventing ways to do things. She sees her best moments in the classroom as those when her mind is "being stretched . . . by kids' questions, by new discoveries. Like I feel different, I feel like I've grown at the end."

Luisa has thrived over the years, taking on a leadership role as a mentor teacher and cooperating teacher, and pursuing professional development activities. Like Kay, she tends to look at challenges as problems to solve and has an experimental mindset about her work. For example, when a new teacher across the hall complained that his students didn't listen to him, Luisa asked, "What did you learn about them today?"

Like Angela, Luisa needs to feel that she belongs. It is an important value from childhood and is reflected in the kind of community she tries to create as a teacher. Luisa's experiences as a Hispanic girl are prominent in her reflections about teaching and are connected to her own belief about school and classroom communities where there is sympathetic understanding and appreciation for differences. Teaching seems to suit Luisa, and her school is a good fit, allowing her to grow in ways consistent with her beliefs.

COMPARING INFLUENCES ON TEACHER DEVELOPMENT

Angela, Luisa, and Kay are all highly intelligent women who decided to teach. It is reasonable to suppose that such women will expect that whatever profession they enter will provide them with a source of intellectual stimulation and allow them to continue to grow. In fact, this may be the most striking difference between the experiences of the three. There are other significant differences, however. As we shall see, both Kay and Luisa experienced continuity of experience, supportive environments, and opportunities for leadership that Angela did not experience.

Professional Support

Luisa and Kay have been in environments that support their intellectual engagement in the profession of teaching and challenge them to grow. This is not how Angela has experienced her various school environments. Both Luisa and Kay had support from the program during their entry years. Kay was part of the PDS and constantly rubbing shoulders with TC faculty, supervisors, students, and graduates who were teaching at her school. When Luisa found herself thwarted in the school in the Bronx, she had several conversations with preservice faculty. She occasionally participated in activities of the New Teacher Recruitment and Retention Project that she had worked for while she was a student. She was visited occasionally by a supervisor from the New Teacher Project. Luisa was able to critique the structures of her school situation, rather than blaming herself or the profession for the failings of her particular school.

Angela, who had not developed close peer relationships during the preservice program, was isolated in a boarding school. Although a support group for beginning teachers (made up of peers who had been in the program with her) met weekly at TC, she was too far away to participate. And while there were people who were helpful to her in making the adjustment to the boarding school, it was, perhaps, easy enough to begin questioning her career choice. Communities of support, which both Luisa and Kay experienced, did not seem to be available to Angela in her search for the kind of continuous learning, reflective thinking, and experimental approach to teaching and learning that she desired.

Intellectual Engagement

Dewey (1933) pointed out that *"upon its intellectual side education consists in the formation of wide-awake, careful, thorough habits of thinking"* (pp. 248–249; emphasis in original). But for the teacher to be able to remain wide awake to the possibilities for children, and for self-development, the school must support teaching as an intellectual activity. Much of the school and curriculum reform efforts of past decades failed because policy makers and reformers neglected to take into account the teacher's vital intellectual role. And teaching has not had a strong holding power for academically able, well-educated, and highly articulate individuals because it has not offered them work that demands use of these gifts. Angela looked elsewhere. She found in law school the kind of rigorous, challenging intellectual environment she needed, but the practice of law did not offer her the satisfaction that she experienced in teaching, despite the constraints she felt. So she tried again, and again found herself head to head with the system.

Collaboration

Intellectual engagement is strengthened by positive collaboration. While many schools offer collegial environments, they are not always characterized by positive, democratic cooperation and collaborative activity. Students in the preservice program are taught how to use democratic group process and cooperative learning in the classroom and how to work in collaboration with peers. Most seek out opportunities for collaboration during their beginning years as teachers.

As soon as Kay realized she would be teaching fourth grade following her internship, she sought out another teacher, Jason, and they began working together on the curriculum. This has been a pattern for her ever since. On a typical day Kay can be found seated around a table with a group of teachers after school working on curriculum. Kay's involvement with a group of grade-level peers has kept her thinking about her own practice.

In contrast, Angela's discussion about collaborative planning focuses on one experience with one third-grade teacher. She talks about collaboration as "nice" and something that makes work easier, but there seem to have been few instances of real collaboration in any of her school settings.

Luisa, on the other hand, has not had as many experiences in across-grade-level collaboration because of the small school size. She has had many student teachers with whom she seems to collaborate, however. But whether or not Luisa has the experience of doing collaborative planning for her classroom, she is in a collaborative environment where colleagues hold meaningful discussions about issues that matter.

Curriculum Decision Making

All three women have experience in curriculum development. Kay has had more experience in collaborative curriculum development than either Luisa or Angela. The planning group mentioned above was primarily focused on curriculum development, though many other issues of teaching and learning came to the table in discussions. The relationship of teachers to curriculum development and implementation is one of the primary ways in which teachers are either challenged and stretched intellectually, or deskilled.

Perhaps most schools see a role for teachers in curriculum decision making, but it is usually that of intelligent adaptation of the strategies suggested in an adopted curriculum. In this way it can be customized for a local context based on the teacher's greater knowledge of specific students, the local community, and available resources. However, academically able teachers who have expertise in curriculum design, assessment, and critique may want more from the profession. When they can find enough room for creativity through adapting the mandated curriculum, they may be able to find teaching satisfying enough.

But in many, many classrooms, there is a much more restrictive orientation to the teacher's role that is exacerbated by the politics of high-stakes testing. Curriculum that is highly prescriptive places the teacher in the role of technician. The current technological orientation mandates methods and reduces the teacher's role to that of establishing a working climate within the classroom and selecting from given strategies that seem most suitable for a particular group of students. The result strips "teachers of their professionalism and undermines the attainment of excellence in the long run" (Zumwalt, 1988, p. 169).

Luisa and Angela have both been engaged in curriculum development activities and value the experience they gained in their preservice program. But, despite her remarkable success with an interdisciplinary curriculum that addressed important environmental issues, Angela believes that she has been in few places where she felt the freedom to develop and teach the curriculum she chooses. Luisa and Kay, on the other hand, have felt much more freedom. Angela has experienced teaching as a constant fight to create opportunities to contribute to the school and the profession. Luisa and Kay have been part of schools where the culture is oriented toward professionalism and where their role as curriculum decision makers has been valued.

Involvement With Parents

Another striking difference in the experiences of the three teachers has to do with parent involvement in the classroom. We have seen how Kay has involved parents in her curriculum. In listening to Angela's reflections on her career, she does not talk about parent involvement in the way Luisa and Kay talk about it. Angela has been a child advocate and undoubtedly works closely with parents through her tutoring agency. But she does not talk about parents as part of her school and classroom experience. Luisa, on the other hand, talks about how parents have had a strong impact on shaping her practice.

> It comes from dropping my brother off at high school, his first day . . . you know, I'm basically his parent. . . . He went in and I started crying and crying. I have to trust that all these strange people in this building are going to do this good job for him. And I don't know them, I haven't met them, I don't know what kind of day he's gonna have. So he goes away all happy to get away from me, and I'm standing in the street, crying. And it just made me think that's what parents feel all the time when they leave their kids with me . . . the trust they're giving me is just amazing. And I feel like I have to live up to that, you know.

Like Angela, Luisa sometimes chafes under the image of teaching and feels that parents do not always respect the work of teachers in the way they should. But she feels an empathy with them, as well as accountability for the education of their children. And her school emphasizes parental involvement, much as does Kay's school.

Assumption of Leadership

Another, perhaps less apparent, difference in the careers of the three has to do with teacher leadership, one of the themes of the TC preservice program. Both Kay and Luisa began to assume leadership responsibilities early in their careers. Leadership was a key motivation for Luisa in her choice of teaching as a career, and she equates the role of teacher with that of a leader. Luisa became involved in the New Teacher Recruitment Project while she was a student, assuming leadership in various events held at undergraduate colleges and in mentoring minority students at TC. In her school, teachers see themselves as leaders and assume responsibility for running the school. One of the frustrations of her first year was her discovery that she had something to give—but that nobody seemed to be interested in learning from or with her.

This seems to be a career-long frustration for Angela. She sees teaching as an important intellectual activity. She sees herself as engaged in a constant battle to get other people interested in things she believes to be crucial, whether it has to do with children's learning or adults redressing system failures.

Like Angela, Kay is concerned about creating policies that affect the lives of children and the school. But Kay found a venue within her school that supports involvement.

> The first couple of years I really just felt like I had to deal with my own classroom. . . . I realized, "you know if you're there you get to have a say. If you're not, you don't." . . . I always thought, you know [the principal] or somebody else made all the decisions.

School-based management became a forum for her.

> After that, I think I just sort of pushed my way into a lot more situations that would put me in a place where I could at least hear what they were talking about even if I didn't stick my two cents in. It's very hard for me to sit somewhere and not stick my two cents in.

Kay became deeply involved in the PDS. Her first role was as part of the PDS faculty who have student teachers and interns and meet periodically to discuss PDS issues. She took a course held on site at her school, focusing on the role of the cooperating teacher. She also became part of a group at her school that decided to develop milestones expected of interns. Later, the teachers did action research about how to help student teachers make a smooth transition from first to second semester. The group met for a semester, with support from a preservice faculty member. And Kay became the first graduate of the program to become a member of the clinical faculty in the program, serving for 2 years. As clinical faculty, she was part of the core planning, teaching, and evaluation team. And each semester as clinical faculty, she shepherded a group of preservice students, providing feedback on their reflection papers and core assignments, pushing them to become self-critical and reflective.

CONCLUSION

If Angela and Kay, or Angela and Luisa, had changed places in their early years of teaching, would there have been a different outcome to their individual teaching stories? Had Luisa remained in the Bronx, would she have "bought in" to the pedagogy of poverty Haberman (1991) describes? How much of the career trajectory of each has had to do with chance? How much with personality and individual choice? These are not questions we can answer. But it seems safe to say that there are factors present in the experiences of Luisa and Kay that Angela did not have. Perhaps the primary factors are continuity of experience, supportive school environments, and opportunities for leadership. These have allowed Kay and Luisa to continue to develop as intellectuals within a school environment while Angela has had to find her place in education outside the school.

Kay and Luisa have found a way to make teaching intellectually satisfying. In talking with them, observing them in action, and reading their written work, it is striking to see that both are able to reframe the ambiguities and challenges of being in the classroom, life as a teacher, and the politics of school—all are posed in the form of problems to be addressed. Both Kay and Luisa have been able to balance the rewards and frustrations of teaching in a way that works.

∽ 9 ∾

To Dwell in Possibility

WE ENTERED Kay's story with a poem by Emily Dickinson:

> I dwell in Possibility
> A fairer house than Prose,
> More numerous of windows,
> Superior of doors.

Throughout the story, Kay is wide awake to the possibilities of a profession that will allow her to live out her deepest values. Some of her values are discovered over time as she is prompted to think about herself, what she knows, how she has come to know it, and what its meaning is for her now.

One of the arguments that has been front and center in teacher education is about what ought to be the knowledge base for teachers. While there are many things worth knowing through teacher education, Kay's story has not raised questions about the knowledge base of teaching. It has been far more concerned with how meaning is constructed from various modes of coming to know.

There is a place for discussion of the appropriate knowledge base of teaching. However, such discussions too frequently reduce teaching to the act of applying or transmitting knowledge and best ways to do this in schools. Dwayne Huebner (1985) has argued that one of the problems with schools is that they "are not places of knowing, but places of knowledge" (p. 172). Knowledge suggests being informed, understanding things, having wisdom, and being enlightened. Knowledge focuses us on bodies of accumulated information and principles. Coming to know suggests meaning-making that draws on bodies of accumulated information and principles but also draws on multiple sources of meaning, including prior knowledge and practical experience.

POSSIBILITIES FOR KAY

We have been watching Kay as she comes to know through making sense of her experiences, a process that suggests intelligent, wise, profound participation in life. Beginning with what she already knows, Kay has been invited into reflective action that includes but is not limited to teacher education knowledge. To really think about what she knows in such a way that she can name it, deconstruct it, and live with the discomfort of reconstruction, Kay has had to call upon her intellectual, physical, emotional, and spiritual self. There is no formula for her to follow as she dwells on what she knows and the possibilities inherent in it. To "dwell in possibility" is to participate in the transcendent. The process is never finished; it is a creative action. Dwelling invites possibilities that include waiting and being, as well as acting. Inspiration, intuition, insight, and synthesis are ways of knowing that require pause and reflection—deliberation. Deliberation is not time-efficient if it is measured by the clock or calendar. It is not certain or uniform in the way many educators would like teacher preparation to be certain. But it invites a future of hope and expectancy.

Without possibility, hope, and expectancy, Kay's story would be a dull story. Instead, it is filled with life and interest. In reading her story, we have participated in her life. We will leave her story, but it continues without us. As this book is concluding, she has become tenured in her new school, following a maternity leave. Kay's twins are celebrating their first birthday. Being a parent is a new kind of dwelling in possibilities for her. "Now as a mom who has much less time on her hands," she reflects, "I am reexamining [teaching] again to see what is necessary and what I do that really makes an impact on the kids." We can anticipate that parenting will open whole new ways of looking at her teaching craft. Teaching can be a profession that invites her again, welcoming her into the classroom with other possibilities for using her experience.

POSSIBILITIES FOR TEACHER EDUCATION

We have learned many lessons from Kay as we have moved through her story. Her story suggests that there is a vital role for university-based teacher preparation in setting up the dialectical relationship between knowledge and coming to know, cultural history and knowledge and pedagogy. University preparation can and should lay the intellectual groundwork that will keep teaching interesting and challenging. This groundwork has to include more than what we have thought of as the knowledge base of teaching. A more powerful emphasis will be on processes of knowing and construction of meaning out of personal, official, and practical knowledge.

For this to happen, universities need to rethink their traditional modes of preparing teachers. As much as we might wish that every teacher could have an opportunity as rich as the one Kay had, with the luxury of student teaching and an internship, it is not realistic to imagine that it will become common practice. Yet teacher education programs, like the one at TC, have a continuing role to play. Teacher education programs should be reshaped to match the realities of teacher supply and demand, while drawing on the very real expertise of their graduates.

Teachers like Kay, Luisa, and Angela have been prepared to be deliberative leaders in the field. By the time most TC preservice program graduates are well into their first year of teaching, they have assumed leadership roles at their school, usually in leading curriculum development groups or teaching workshops on various models of teaching. Given periodic cycles of teacher shortage, in which classrooms are filled with unqualified teachers, it makes sense to think about how to build on the leadership potential of teachers such as Kay. Kay's inclination to pull together beginning teachers and teachers on grade level to talk about curriculum issues could become an intentional activity for teachers who have been prepared along similar lines. Their role in the induction of new, less well-prepared teachers could be intellectually challenging for everyone involved.

Whatever form teacher education takes in the future, the university should not give up its separate role from that of the schools. Although it is critical that there be intensive, collaborative work in schools, and although many courses that now constitute a part of university-based teacher education could be taught in local school centers, there is also something to be said for being away from the school. Meeting at the university removes student teachers from the action of the classroom and can help them learn how to see in new ways. Disciplines of knowledge, study of how children learn, and methods of teaching become lenses through which practice can be viewed in new ways—ways that are not possible in the thick of classroom action. Movement between schools and universities can and should include teachers and administrators as well. The study of teaching should involve a constant, interactive movement between sites and among faculties of schools and universities.

POSSIBILITIES FOR SCHOOLS

School districts need to rethink how teachers are welcomed into the profession. Assigning mentors to new teachers makes very little sense unless mentors are able to build on the experiences that teacher education graduates bring with them. Just as universities have been guilty of thinking about how to demolish prior knowledge of teaching in order to replace it with official teacher education knowledge, school districts have been guilty of treating new teachers as if they have had no prior preparation or experience. Staff development days are "treatment" days in which teachers are told about methods or new curricula and how to implement them. Kay's story suggests that academically able teachers have to be involved in the intellectual activities of curriculum and teaching and not relegated to the role of implementing someone else's idea of what children need to know. A more powerful model of staff development will include briefings on new knowledge, research, or public demands that have implications for curriculum reform. It will recognize that teachers have different levels of interest and background preparation and will invite those who have a more experimental mindset to engage in curriculum inquiry around new knowledge, research, or public demands. Schools as communities of inquiry support and sustain deliberative teachers.

POSSIBILITIES FOR THE FUTURE

The media and popular press are engaged in a constant debate about how to improve the quality of education and have been—with more or less intensity—for decades. The public debate begs the question that has been central to the story of Kay: How can we prepare, support, and sustain deliberative teachers? The public debate usually focuses on cognitive knowledge and skills that teachers ought to have and children should be learning. But a hopeful future also requires that schools of our society attend to the development of essential capacities such as *wonder*, which leads to poetry, art, invention, and recognition of the transcendent in human experience; *reflection*, which leads to synthesis of diverse fields of information, creativity, problem posing and solving, inner peace, thoughtful action, and wisdom; *merriment*, which leads to a balanced perspective on life and to appreciation and critique of ourselves and our world; *friendship*, which enlarges our capacity for justice, responsibility, and caring, defending us from physical, mental, and spiritual loneliness and isolation; and *compassion*, which makes it possible for us to be with others in their pain and approach them as friend rather than enemy. To prepare children for a hopeful future, teachers must be able to do more than implement a handful of strategies they have learned in a teacher education program or on the job. They must have an experimental mindset and be equipped to study situations and invent appropriate solutions by drawing on multiple sources of information and materials. These are the skills of deliberative teaching, and they are won through constant, continuous reconstruction of experience.

References

Abdal-Haqq, I. (1998). *Professional development schools: Weighing the evidence.* Thousand Oaks, CA: Corwin Press.

Adler, A. (1964). *The individual psychology of Alfred Adler: A systematic presentation in selections from his writings* (H. L. Ansbacher & R. R. Ansbacher, Eds.). New York: Harper Colophon Books, Harper & Row. (Original works published 1904–1944)

Apple, M. (1982). *Education and power.* New York: Routledge & Kegan Paul.

Arnstine, B. (1990). Rational and caring teachers: Restructuring teacher-preparation. *Teachers College Record, 32*(3), 24–25.

Bettleheim, B. (1987). *A good enough parent: A book on child-rearing.* New York: Vintge Books.

Beyer, L. (1984). Field experience and ideology and the development of critical reflectivity. *Journal of Teacher Education, 35*(3), 36–41.

Bolin, F. S. (1987). The teacher as curriculum decision maker. In F. S. Bolin & J. M. Falk (Eds.), *Teacher renewal: Professional issues, personal choices* (pp. 92–108). New York: Teachers College Press.

Bolin, F. S. (1988). Helping student teachers think about teaching. *Journal of Teacher Education, 39*(2), 48–55.

Bolin, F. S. (1990). Student teacher thinking: Another look at Lou. *Journal of Teacher Education, 41*(1), 10–19.

Bolin, F. S. (1994). Introduction: Getting going, staying on. In R. Sawyer (Ed.), *Building on diversity: Exploring issues of teacher retention* (Monograph) (pp. 2–8). New Teacher Recruitment and Retention Project, Teachers College, Columbia University, New York.

Britzman, D. P. (1986). Cultural myths in the making of a teacher: Biography and social structure in teacher education. *Harvard Education Review, 56*(4), 442–456.

Calderhead, J. (1996). Teachers: Beliefs and knowledge. In D. C. Berliner & R. C. Calfee (Eds.), *Handbook of educational psychology* (pp. 709–725). New York: Macmillan.

Calderhead, J., & Robson, M. (1991). Images of teaching: Student teachers' early conceptions of classroom practice. *Teaching and Teacher Education, 7*(1), 1–8.

Clark, C. M. (1988). Asking the right questions about teacher-preparation: Contributions of research on teacher thinking. *Educational Researcher, 17*(2), 5–12.

Cochran-Smith, M. (2000). Teacher education at the turn of the century [Editorial]. *Journal of Teacher Education, 51*(3), 163–165.

Cochran-Smith, M. L., & Lytle, S. L. (2001). Beyond certainty: Taking an inquiry stance on practice. In A. M. Lieberman & L. Miller (Eds.), *Teachers caught in the action: Professional development that matters* (pp. 44–55). New York: Teachers College Press.

Cruickshank, D., & Applegate, J. (1981). Reflective teaching as a strategy for teacher growth. *Educational Leadership, 38*(7), 553–554.

Dewey, J. (1904). The relation of theory to practice in education. In R. D. Archambault (Ed.), *John Dewey on education: Selected writings* (pp. 313–338). Chicago: University of Chicago Press.

Dewey, J. (1933). The process and product of reflective activity: Psychological process and logical form. In R. D. Archambault (Ed.), *John Dewey on education: Selected writings* (pp. 242–249). Chicago: University of Chicago Press.

Elliott, J. (1976–77). Developing hypotheses about classrooms from teachers' practical constructs: An account of the work of the Ford Teaching Project. *Interchange, 7*(2), 2–22.

Freire, P. (1999). *Pedagogy of the oppressed*. New York: Continuum. (Original work published 1970)

Glickman, C., & Gordon, S. P. (1987). Clarifying developmental supervision. *Educational Leadership, 44*(8), 64–70.

Goodlad, J. I. (1997). *In praise of education*. New York: Teachers College Press.

Goodman, J. (1988). Constructing a practical philosophy of teaching: A study of preservice teachers' professional perspectives. *Teaching and Teacher Education, 4*(2), 121–137.

Grierson, P. C. (1974, Summer). The "Humpty-Dumpty" of educational theory and practice. *Education for Teaching, 95*, 39–46.

Griffin, G. A. (1986). Clinical teacher education. In J. Hoffman & S. Edwards (Eds.), *Reality and reform in clinical teacher education* (pp. 1–23). New York: Random House.

Haberman, M. (1991). The pedagogy of poverty versus good teaching. *Phi Delta Kappan, 73*(4), 290–294.

Hollingsworth, S. (1989). Prior beliefs and cognitive change in learning to teach. *American Educational Research Journal, 26*(2), 160–189.

Huebner, D. (1985). Spirituality and knowing. In E. Eisner (Ed.), *Learning and teaching the ways of knowing: Eighty-fourth yearbook of the National Society for the Study of Education* (pp. 159–173). Chicago: University of Chicago Press.

Jersild, A. (1955). *When teachers face themselves*. New York: Teachers College Press.

Joram, E., & Gabriele, A. J. (1998). Preservice teachers' prior beliefs: Transforming obstacles into opportunities. *Teaching and Teacher Education, 14*(2), 175–191.

Kagan, D. M. (1992). Professional growth among preservice and beginning teachers. *Review of Educational Research, 62*(2), 129–169.

Knapp, M. S., et al. (1995). *Teaching for meaning in high poverty classrooms*. New York: Teachers College Press.

Lampert, M., & Clark, A. J. (1990). Expert knowledge and expert thinking in teaching: A response to Floden and Klinzing. *Educational Researcher, 19*(4), 21–23.

Lortie, D. (1975). *Schoolteacher: A sociological study*. Chicago: University of Chicago Press.

Macdonald, J. B. (1975). Curriculum theory. In W. Pinar (Ed.), *Curriculum theorizing* (pp. 3–16). Berkeley, CA: McCutchan.

Maslow, A. (1968). *Toward a psychology of being*. Princeton, NJ: Van Nostrand.

Maxson, M., & Sindelar, R. (1998). Images revisited: Examining preservice teachers' ideas about teaching. *Teacher Education Quarterly, 25*(2), 5–26.

McNeil, L. M. (1986). *Contradictions of control: School structure and school knowledge*. New York: Routledge.

Moore, T. (Ed.). (1997). *The education of the heart*. New York: Harper Perennial.

Murnane, R. R. (1991). *Who will teach? Policies that matter*. Cambridge, MA: Harvard University Press.

Pritchard, F., & Ancess, J. (1999). *The effects of professional development schools: A literature review*. New York: National Center on Restructuring Education, Schools, and Teaching, Teachers College, Columbia University.

Pultorak, E. G. (1993). Facilitating reflective thought in novice teachers. *Journal of Teacher Education, 44*(3), 288–295.

Rodriguez, A. J. (1993). A dose of reality: Understanding the origin of the theory/practice dichotomy in teacher education from the students' point of view. *Journal of Teacher Education, 44*(3), 213–222.

Schoonmaker, F. (2001). Curriculum making, models, practices and issues: A knowledge fetish? In L. Corno (Ed.), *Education across a century: The centennial volume: One hundredth yearbook of the National Society for the Study of Education*, Part I. (pp. 1–33). Chicago: University of Chicago Press.

Shulman, L. (1987). Knowledge and teaching: Foundations of the new reform. *Harvard Education Review, 57*(1), 1–22.

Smyth, J. (1989). Developing and sustaining critical reflection in teacher education. *Journal of Teacher Education, 40*(2), 2–9.

Snyder, J. (1992). Documentation of the first three years of the District Three/United Federation of Teachers/Teachers College Professional Development School Project. New York: Report to the Ford Foundation.

Snyder, J. (1994). Perils and potentials: A tale of two professional development schools. In L. Darling-Hammond (Ed.), *Professional development schools* (pp. 98–125). New York: Teachers College Press.

Sparks-Langer, G. M., & Colton, A. B. (1991). Synthesis of research on teachers' reflective thinking. *Educational Leadership, 48*(6), 37–44.

Sparks-Langer, G. M., & Simmons, J. M. (1990). Reflective pedagogical thinking: How can we promote it and measure it? *Journal of Teacher Education, 41*(4), 23–32.

Tabachnick, B. R., & Zeichner, K. M. (1984). The impact of the student-teaching experience on the development of teacher perspectives. *Journal of Teacher Education, 35*(6), 28–36.

Tom, A. (1985, March–April). *Inquiry into teacher education*. Paper presented at the meeting of the American Educational Research Association, Chicago.

Van Manen, M. (1977). Linking ways of knowing with ways of being practical. *Curriculum Inquiry, 6*(3), 205–228.

Wildman, T. M., & Niles, J. A. (1987). Reflective teachers: Tensions between abstractions and realities. *Journal of Teacher Education, 38*(4), 25–31.

Yinger, R., & Clark, C. (1981). *Reflective journal writing: Theory and practice.* East Lansing: Michigan State University Institute for Research on Teaching.

Zeichner, K. M. (1980). Myths and realities: Field-based experiences in preservice teacher education. *Journal of Teacher Education, 31*(6), 45–55.

Zeichner, K. M. (1984, January–February). *The ecology of field experience: Toward an understanding of the role of field experiences in teacher development.* Paper presented at the annual meeting of the Association of Teacher Educators, New Orleans.

Zeichner, K. M. (1987). Preparing reflective teachers: An overview of instructional strategies which have been employed in preservice teacher education. *International Journal of Educational Research, 11*(5), 565–575.

Zeichner, K. M., & Liston, D. P. (1987). Teaching student teachers to reflect. *Harvard Educational Review, 57*(1), 23–48.

Zeichner, K. M., & Tabachnick, B. R. (1981). Are the effects of university teacher education "washed out" by school experience? *Journal of Teacher Education, 32*(3), 7–10.

Zumwalt, K. K. (1982). Research on teaching: Policy implications for teacher education. In A. Lieberman & M. W. McLaughlin (Eds.), *Policy making in education: Eighty-first yearbook of the National Society for the Study of Education, Part I* (pp. 215–248). Chicago: University of Chicago Press.

Zumwalt, K. K. (1988). Are we improving or undermining teaching? In L. N. Tanner (Ed.), *Critical issues in curriculum: Eighty-seventh yearbook of the National Society for the Study of Education, Part I.* Chicago: University of Chicago Press.

Index

Abdal-Haqq, I., 80
Achievements. *See* Honors/achievements
Action research, 6, 10, 132
Adler, Alfred, 17, 18-19
Agency, 23–25, 34–36
Ancess, J., 62–63, 66, 67, 80, 81
Angela (teacher), 119–24, 128–33, 136
Apple, M., 5
Applegate, J., 8
Arnstine, B., 5, 107
At risk, being, 5–7, 15–16, 84, 107, 118

Barriers to teaching, 1, 3–7, 11–14, 84–100, 101, 118, 124
Bettlcheim, B., 35
Beyer, L., 8
Bolin, F. S., 8, 10, 21, 47, 49, 103, 124, 126
Boring lessons, 53, 54, 58–59, 60, 73, 123
Brenda (student teacher), 85, 86, 88, 94, 103, 104, 106, 114, 115
Britzman, D. P., 4, 5, 14, 15, 20, 48, 59, 99, 102, 107

Calderhead, J., 4, 20
Candice (student teacher), 85, 87–88, 89–90, 91, 93, 94, 95, 96, 104, 105, 106, 108–9, 114
Child-centeredness, 103–4
China. *See* Cross-cultural recollections
Christy (student), 56, 58–59
Clark, A. J., 8
Clark, C., 3, 4, 8, 20
Classrooms: and barriers to teaching, 84, 85–88, 95; environment of, 34, 36, 41, 42, 84, 85–88, 95, 126; negative recollections of, 34, 36, 41, 42. *See also* Control
Clinical faculty, 6, 68–69, 117, 132–33
Cochran-Smith, M. L., 103, 108
Cognition, 8, 9, 21

Collaboration/cooperation: and barriers to teaching, 93–95; building, 93–95; and clinical faculty, 68–69; and constant and consistent dialectic, 106, 111, 114; and continuous learning, 123, 129; and control, 111, 114; and curriculum development, 114–17, 118, 136; and deconstructing personal knowledge, 14–15; and "growing up" PDS, 81–82, 114–15, 116–17, 118; and internship, 79, 80; and learning as continuous reconstruction, 129–30; and owning knowledge, 66, 72; and PDS goals, 15; and PDS partnership, 62, 63; and possibilities, 136; and professional community, 83; and teacher development as socialization, 5. *See also* Cooperating teachers; Cooperative learning
"College as savior" myth, 70–71
Colton, A. B., 8, 9
Commanding presence, 88–89, 101
Common sense, 105–6
Community/communities: developing professional, 62–83; and possibilities, 137
Constructivism, 4, 46, 47, 69, 78, 91, 92
Continuous learning, 62, 71, 104–6, 117, 119–33
Control: and barriers to teaching, 12, 84, 101, 107–14; and collaboration, 111; and constant and consistent dialectic, 101, 106, 107–14; and curriculum, 112–14; and fun, 45, 46–47, 53, 54–55; and owning knowledge, 74; and "pedagogy of poverty," 3; and persistence of personal knowledge, 52–57, 60–61; redefining, 54–57; and significance of personal knowledge, 57, 58; and teacher development as socialization, 5
Cooperating teachers: for Kay, 5, 6, 67–68, 71–72, 74–75, 77, 82, 83; and Kay as

About the Author

FRANCES SCHOONMAKER is a professor of education in the Department of Curriculum and Teaching, Teachers College, Columbia University, where she served as codirector of the Preservice Program in Childhood Education from 1983 to 2001. She received her Ed.D. from Teachers College, Columbia University. Professor Schoonmaker was reared in Oklahoma, the daughter of schoolteachers. She came to academe with 15 years of elementary school teaching experience in Washington, Oregon, Tennessee, and Maryland. She has written extensively on the teacher's role in curriculum decision making and the historical and contextual factors that have supported and impeded this role. Professor Schoonmaker has taught in China and Japan and is Concurrent Professor in the Institute on Moral Education at Nanjing Normal University in China.